Copyright 2018 by Nori Dinahan. All rights reserved. No part of this publication may be reproduced or transmitted in any form or by any means, graphic, electronic or mechanical, including photocopying, recording or any information storage and retrieval system, without permission in writing from the publisher.

Library and Archives Canada Cataloguing in Publication

Dinahan, Lance, Author, 1961, Author
LaFonte, Norma, Author, 1958, Author
  Money Monster or Money Master? Teach your kids the basics of money and have them love every minute: money, parents, children, kids, spending
Issued also in electronic format
ISBN # 978-0-9921609-1-3
Kids - Finance, Money, Entrepreneur, Wealth, Financial education.
Adult – Finance, Money, Wealth, Debt, Entrepreneur, Wealth, Financial Education
Cover Design by Fusion Creative Works
Publisher: The True Wealth Group

The following information is intended as a general reference tool for understanding the underlying principles and practises of the subject matter covered. The opinions and ideas expressed herein are solely those of the authors. The authors and publishers are not engaged in rendering legal, accounting, tax, insurance, financial, investment or other professional advice or services in this publication. The publication is not intended to provide a basis for action in any circumstances without consideration by a competent professional. The strategies outlined in this book may not be suitable for every individual and are not guaranteed or warrantied to produce any particular result. Further, any examples or sample forms represented are intended only as illustrations.

The author, publisher and their agents assume no responsibility for errors or omissions and expressly disclaim any responsibility for any liability, loss or risk, personal or other-wise, which is incurred as a consequence, directly or indirectly of the use and application of any of the contents of this book.

All inquiries should be addressed to:
YET – Young Entrepreneur Training/Money Monster or Money Master
34159 Kirkpatrick Ave, Mission, BC V2V 0B4
Phone: 1-855- 938-5437 or 1-855-YET-Kids
www.MoneyMonsterorMoneyMaster.com

Facebook Page: MoneyMonsterorMoneyMaster?

Bulk Purchases: If you are interested in bulk purchases of *MONEY MONSTER OR MONEY MASTER? Teach Your Kids the Basics of Money and Have Them Love Every Minute*, we offer an aggressive discount schedule. Quantity discounts are available to companies, educational institutes or financial service organizations for re-selling, educational purposes, subscription incentives, gifts or fundraiser campaigns. Please call us at one of the above numbers.

Our Book's Vision:

To Inspire People of All Ages to Become Financially Aware

Our Mission:

To Encourage Adults to Open a Dialog with Kids about Money and Create Financial Responsibility through Conversation

To Develop Financial Confidence and a Life of True Wealth – Where Each Person Can Live a Life of Choice

Our Values:

Respect
Integrity
Responsibility
Accountability
Service

Table of Contents

Introduction: What Is a Money Monster?

Part 1

Chapter 1: Money Talks

Chapter 2: So Where Do Kids Learn about Money?

Chapter 3: Find a Mentor

Part 2

Chapter 4: Why Should You Listen to Us?

Chapter 5: Lance's Story

Chapter 6: Lance's Gumball Kid

Chapter 7: Norma's Story

Chapter 8: The Universe Provides Lessons

Part 3

Chapter 9: A Kid's Perspective on Money

Chapter 10: Where Does Money Come From?

Chapter 11: Managing Systems

Chapter 12: Kids and Allowances

Chapter 13: Allowance Money for Chores

Chapter 14: Allowance for Money Management

Chapter 15: Wants and Needs

Part 4

Chapter 16: Money Master Management—

Mmm . . .

Everyone Loves a Good Thing That Makes Life

Sweeter!

Chapter 17: Necessities of Life Jar

Chapter 18: Save to Spend Jar

Chapter 19: Education Jar

Chapter 20: Play Jar

Chapter 21: Wealth Jar

Chapter 22: Give Jar

Part 5

Chapter 23: Allowance Hour with Lance

Chapter 24: Do Your Kids Really Use Jars?

Chapter 25: The Allure of Credit

Chapter 26: Kids and Credit Cards

Chapter 27: Should You Allow Your Kid to Have a

Debit or Credit Card?

Chapter 28: Debit Card Rules

Chapter 29: Credit Card Rules

Chapter 30: Loaning Money to Kids

Part 6

Chapter 31: Mmm Sounds Good—How Can I Make It Work in My Money Monster-Filled Life?

Chapter 32: What Is the First Step for Moving Forward?

Chapter 33: Lower Your Expenses

Chapter 34: Increase Cash Flow

Chapter 35: Insanity

Chapter 36: Financially Overwhelmed? Know You Need to Take Action?

Chapter 37: Pay Yourself First to Reach Financial Freedom

Chapter 38: Passive Income

Chapter 39: Passive Income and the Rat Race

Chapter 40: Wealth Ratios

Chapter 41: Influence from Others

Chapter 42: Finding a Personal Mentor

Chapter 43: It's Time to Teach Your Kids

Chapter 44: The Mmm and the YET Program – Kids' Perspectives

Chapter 45: Final Thoughts

Part 7

Additional Resources and Information

Introduction
What Is a Money Monster?

Society creates Money Monsters. A Money Monster helps people live in the moment without thinking about the future. He looks friendly, and he really is easy to find when you don't really need him. He should be easily tamed; after all, he's fed on a monthly payment plan. He's fun to own and allows you to do things you might not yet have the money to do, or buy things you may need or want but don't have the money for right now.

You may have already guessed: The Money Monster is credit which often turns into bad debt.

He may come dressed up as a Credit Card, a Bank Loan, a Car Payment, or even a Quick Pay Day Loan. Sadly, he can quickly grow out of control . . . for instance, if you cannot feed him a full meal, or if you feed him late. Worse yet, get him a few friends to hang out with. Money Monster appetites grow quickly when grouped together. Soon you begin to hate the Money Monster, but you can't seem to get him out of your life. He needs more and more money to keep him fed. If you stop feeding him, everything you have worked so hard for may be lost.

Wait. Did we just describe your life?

Don't worry if we did—it's not all your fault. You were not likely given the tools you needed when you were younger. If you were never given the tools to tame a Money Monster, it only makes sense you can't share the tools with your kids either.

For years, most people have been pressured by society to go to school, get good grades, get a good job, and live life to the fullest. Even if it means buying on credit. Buy it today and pay for it tomorrow! Cars, clothes, furniture, vacations, you name it. Almost anything you can think of is readily available with the swipe of a card or a signature on a contract.

Lance and I have both learned credit is like a shovel: easy to find, easy to use (no instructions required) but can be a back-breaking tool. Unfortunately, that credit shovel is used by most people to dig themselves deeper and deeper into a hole of debt.

Knowing what the Money Monster is capable of would you encourage your children to own a Money Monster? Of course not. However, society is going to require them to have their own credit at some point in life.

What if you could guide your kids to become a Money Master? A Money Master that can stop the Money Monster in its tracks and use him to their own advantage?

Sounds good, right?

Simply put, we wrote this book because it hurts our hearts when we see people struggle financially. We know they are doing the best they can with what they know; however, if they *knew* better, they would *do* better.

We want to teach people a better way—and to be honest, it's not even hard to do.

We've both made many financial mistakes and we've suffered the consequences. Fortunately, we've also learned a simple money management system that turned our lives around.

We want to change the world one life at a time and we want to start with you and your children.

Our goal is to guide adults to teach kids and stop this cycle of feeding what we call the Money Monster which has become so common for so many. There is no reason on earth our next generations cannot be, do, or have anything they want—without going into bad debt.

This book was written to help create a society of Money Masters—kids who will learn from an early age how to make their money work for them, so they don't ever have to feel the bite of the Money Monster the way most of us have experienced.

Learning to be a Money Master can be done! It all starts with reading this book, applying what you learn with your children and being willing to talk about money as they grow up.

So, are you ready to get started? Let's begin!

Part 1

Chapter 1
Money Talks

An honest and frank discussion around money is a rare occurrence, no matter what age group you are in. For many people growing up, money was either a taboo topic or vague answers were given around the subject.

Did you ever ask your parents how much money they earned? Or even where their source of income came from? If you did ask, it's most likely you were not given a full or honest answer. One reason is, parents think it's not the kid's business to know, or they may be concerned they would tell other people—and no one likes to talk about money. It may have been as simple as they didn't feel like they earned enough, or they were afraid if the kids knew they earned lot of money, they would expect more from Mom and Dad.

The reality is the longer you take to teach your kids about money, the more likely they are to make their own observations and draw their own conclusions. They are likely to learn bad habits over good ones, since they don't hear or see how decisions are made about spending, saving, or investing. All they see is money comes from an ATM or goods are bought with a plastic card.

Our school system is not designed to teach kids the skills and knowledge they need to be successful in life. Teachers rarely address the subject of money in a meaningful way. In some mid-grade schools, a few optional courses on life skills might be offered and these may include learning how to balance a cheque book and set up a budget, but this is too little information and too late to help instill good money management habits. These courses when available, are designed to teach student very basic skills, some of which are becoming obsolete as we write this book. (Does anyone even write a cheque anymore?)

Schools teach kids to think about what they want to do when they graduate high school. They often encourage additional education, such as learning a trade, going to college or university— all to get a good job, with good pay. That's a great idea, but once they graduate and get that great job, they have no idea what to do with the money they receive. They don't have any money management skills.

As adults, we want our kids to be successful, yet we don't teach them how to be successful, particularly in the area of money. We do our best to teach them to be good human beings, but we do very little to teach them how to be good money managers.

Realistically, you can't expect someone to solve a problem if that person doesn't see there is a problem or doesn't have the resources and tools to make changes.

Earning money is relatively easy. If you have a good attitude and are willing to learn, almost anyone can earn money. You don't even really have to be all that talented. There are lots of jobs in this world that require very little talent but will still earn you a paycheque at the end of the day.

Earning money is the easiest part of life. *Managing money* without being taught a money management system is the hard part.

Chapter 2
So Where Do Kids Learn About Money?

Kids are a blank slate when they are born. They don't know love or hate or racism. They don't know good from bad, rich from poor or have any preconceived ideas about anything in life, including money.

Kids not only learn based on what we conscientiously teach them. They also learn by listening, discussion, or simply by modelling behaviors they observe. Intentionally or unintentionally — we teach our kids by our example. Their learning is also impacted by others around them including teachers, neighbors, friends' parents, and other family members, all in the exact same way.

Kids are constantly learning. All. The. Time. Even when they seem to not be paying any attention to what is happening around them. They are like sponges; they soak up everything, including the good, the bad, and the scary.

The Rich Get Richer

It is often said, "The rich get richer and the poor get poorer." We are not sure if that statement is 100 percent true, but we do believe it is partially true—and it's likely because the rich either consciously teach their kids about money and business or the kids learn from overhearing conversations or seeing how wealthy people use money. This is normal—those kids are in an environment where money and business are part of normal, everyday conversations.

Unfortunately, for many poor or middle-class parents, their kids are not exposed to daily conversations or positive observations on those topics. Parents want more for their children, but they are just not able to provide the same kind of environment, or they simply never learned how to manage money and don't know what, or how, to teach.

If a parent or adult was never taught about money or business, it makes sense they cannot share the path to becoming a business owner or entrepreneur or even how to manage their money they earn as employees, so their money can work for them.

Chapter 3
Find a Mentor

Our experiences in life have taught us it is wise to find someone to learn from whenever possible—a mentor or a coach. Find someone who has what you want (a hobby, a skill, a level of wealth, a business) who started where you are at. This person has already made mistakes during their learning process and can share with you what to do—and what not to do.

There is no point in asking a lottery winner or someone who inherited their wealth how to make or manage money . . . unless of course, you hold a winning lottery ticket or expect to inherit a lot of money. If you are lucky enough to find yourself in those shoes, your next step is to make sure that person was successful at keeping their money growing!

Based on statistics, people who suddenly come into large amounts of money are often broke within a few short years. Why? It wasn't from not having enough money—it is simply they didn't know how to manage money, so they blew through it or they hired someone to help them who did not have their best interests at heart.

Likely you are thinking; *Now I have to find a mentor?* The good news is no, you don't. Our first money lessons and mentorship came from reading books by people who had what we wanted, but who had started where we were at that time of our life. One-on-one mentorship is not necessary at this stage of your learning. You can start by finishing this book and then applying these lessons in your own life and in the lives of the children around you.

Most people are honored you believe you can learn from them. Some of our mentors in the past were people we hadn't even met yet. Robert Kiyosaki was one of them. We both had read his book *Rich Dad, Poor Dad* and realized we could learn and apply the knowledge he shared in his book. We didn't need to have a personal relationship with him; we could learn from what we read and then apply his knowledge to our lives. You can do the same.

Money Monster or Money Master? is written in part to be a mentoring book—to help you become a mentor to the people in your life. Even if you don't know the first thing about money, how to look after it, and how to make it grow into a very nice future, we'll show you how.

Additionally, we've learned and implemented a very easy money management system for your kids—and maybe even you—to follow. If you follow the steps outlined throughout the book, your kids will have a brighter future and you could see a huge leap ahead towards your own financial success.

The reality in life is that every successful person has had someone they looked up to or learned from. All people make mistakes along the way, but successful people keep on moving forward and learn from their mistakes. Is the path always smooth and easy? Nope, but it is an adventure—and one worth pursuing to have a better life.

    If you take the opportunity to connect with like-minded people who are on the same path, your journey to success will be much quicker. No matter what you choose to do in life, if you never give up—and we mean NEVER GIVE UP—then SUCCESS will happen for you . . . and for your kids!

Part 2

Chapter 4
Why Should You Listen to Us?

Neither one of us has written about our backgrounds with the intent of bragging about our successes. In fact, in the next few pages you'll see we really don't talk about our own success, other than to establish what is possible for you based on where we started in life.

We both want you to know you can come from any background and become successful. Success is defined differently by different people. We believe if you are happy in your life—and can live a lifestyle that provides you with both happiness and personal fulfillment—you are successful by our definition.

Neither one of us comes from a privileged background. We came from different communities, different social and business backgrounds and no one would consider either one of us particularly, 'lucky' in how we were raised. We each made our own very different mistakes along the way, both personal and financial and yet we both now choose to look at them as learning opportunities instead of allowing them to define our path in life. In short, if we could become successful despite our backgrounds, so can you and the children around you.

One of the topics we will cover going forward is debt—good debt and bad debt. You are probably thinking, *What can possibly be good about debt?* Don't worry, we found that terminology a little confusing when we first heard it too.

Good debt is defined as debt that puts money INTO your pocket, while bad debt is all other debt you have in your life.

A few examples of good debt would be a mortgage owed on a rental property, where the tenants pay all the expenses on the house and there is leftover money to put back in your pocket at the end of each month.

Another example would be money borrowed to make an investment that brings more money in than it takes money out of your pocket, after the cost of servicing the debt itself. The money coming back into your pocket is what we call positive cashflow. Positive cashflow is a good thing.

Bad debt is the opposite. When you have borrowed on credit to make a purchase of any kind, that does not create money coming back to you. For example, a family vacation, a new car, dining out, clothing, and silly as this may sound, even your house mortgage would be considered bad debt by this definition. Don't panic . . . it's perfectly OK with us if you have a home mortgage *if* you can truly afford the payments without sacrificing your quality of life or long-term financial well-being!

What we can share is, life is much easier when you don't have to struggle with bad debt; it is possible to get out of bad debt; and learning to become a Money Master is a choice you can make and find success in. It is not always easy to make changes as an adult—but it is very, very rewarding and life-changing! Not just for you, but for the people around you.

On a commercial aircraft during the safety demonstration, they always tell you to put on your own oxygen mask first in the event of an emergency, so you can then help others. In the next few chapters, you will learn it's important you teach your children to wear an oxygen mask, but you can learn to put one on at the same time. Children learn best by observing and copying the people around them. So whenever possible try to remember that and participate in their learning alongside them.

Chapter 5
Lance's Story

I grew up in a pretty normal home. My parents were good people who respected the money they earned. My mom was a stay-at-home parent and my dad was a small business owner. We had a nice life. We were not rich, nor were we poor, but we never really had enough money to do all the things we wanted to do or buy the stuff we wanted. The topic of money was never discussed in our house—unless it was to talk about things we couldn't afford. Money doesn't grow on trees, you know!

My grandfather owned a small company that painted lines in parking lots and he hired many of his family members to work for him. My dad also owned many small businesses and although he managed to get by, he would not have been considered wealthy by any stretch of the imagination.

And me?

Well, I looked at them and thought, *If I do what they did, I will most likely have what they have.* The problem was I wanted more. A lot more!

The next problem was, I had no idea how to get it. I didn't know or understand about mentorship, so I simply forged ahead and struggled along with lots of different ventures.

I began with a few small, home-based businesses, including reselling items and hiring my friends to work for me. After high school I began to apprentice as an electrician and eventually became a Master Electrician and started my own contracting company.

Along the way, I started to seek more information on how to get rich. I found and read the book *Rich Dad, Poor Dad*, and I soon saw opportunities in the real estate market and began flipping houses in my local community.

I made good money! A lot of money, in fact—so much money I was able to buy many of the things I had always wanted without even really thinking about it.

I also became a spender. A BIG SPENDER! As fast as I made the money, I spent it. Unfortunately, without a money management system, I also became a BIG BAD DEBTOR! Not something I would wish on anyone.

I never managed any of the money I earned. I never saved for a rainy day, nor did I know to set aside a portion of money to invest in my future.

I had the mind-set that the next house I flipped would sell shortly and I would make more money, so I didn't need to think about saving or managing it. I even went as far as to spend the money that was on my line of credit on my personal home. Eventually the market crashed and there were no more houses being sold.

What a nasty wake-up call that was! I no longer had any money in the bank and I knew the real estate market wasn't bouncing back anytime soon. I had a large amount of bad debt, and very little to show for it. The Money Monster had taken a big bite out of my lifestyle and was causing me a lot of stress.

I now understand "The Universe," which some may call "God," was sending me a message. I'm pretty sure the message was: "Well, if you can't manage the money I'm sending your way, then I'll stop giving it to you."

I'm good with money now, but back then I wasn't thinking straight. Fortunately, I was not completely upside down financially. I ended up keeping some of those flip houses and I turned them into cash-flowing assets. Around the same time, I encouraged my teenage son to read *Rich Dad, Poor Dad*. As he read through the book, we would talk about each chapter and what he was learning, and it reminded me, I had fallen from the path I wanted to be on.

Unfortunately, I had wasted a lot of money on both stuff and poor investments. I had "invested" in products, ideas, or people I shouldn't have because I knew nothing about them. If I made a bad investment I figured it would be OK—after all, at the time money was flowing in at a rate that exceeded my expenses.

I also lent money to people I thought were my friends and I did so without written agreements. I just trusted they had the same level of integrity as I did. That wasn't the case, by the way. I learned a lot of hard and expensive life lessons.

I bet you are thinking, *Where were his parents during this time? Why didn't they speak up? What were they doing?*

When I look back, I thought the same thing—why didn't my parents speak up? Why didn't they guide me? Why didn't they step in and say, "Lance, don't waste what you are earning."

I know they could see the mistakes I was making—and in hindsight it likely drove them crazy, but instead of speaking out and calling me on my stupid ways, they shared their concerns behind closed doors with each other. They said things like, "He's too relaxed with his money," and, "He just lets it go too easy."

I don't blame my parents at all. It's not their fault.

Money was not openly discussed as I was growing up—and it became even more of a taboo subject as I became an adult. My parents could not teach what they didn't know. They didn't know how to manage their money for long-term wealth building either. They lived a simple lifestyle and they put a bit of money away for a rainy day, but they never had a lot of extra. They could only share with me what they knew, which was what they learned from their parents and grandparents. I'm sure they thought I wouldn't have listened anyway (and that's probably true).

I believe this is a similar story for most people. We were never taught about money; it simply wasn't a normal part of everyday conversation. Our parents put in an honest day's work for an honest day's pay, but they never really learned how to manage their money in such a way as to have their money work for them! As a result, they couldn't teach us what they didn't know, so honest and open discussions around money were impossible when we were kids.

Chapter 6
Lance's Gumball Kid

As the middle child and our only son, Lucas liked to hang around me, and quite honestly, his mom was happy to have one less child underfoot. So I began to take Lucas to work with me when he was about four-years-old.

Since I knew I wanted to teach my kids about money, I would put him to work fetching tools from the truck or picking up garbage on the job site (this was before he could read about child labor laws), and later as he became more capable, I gave him bigger tasks which taught him some real skills.

I would pay him a little cash and we would speak about money. I taught him what I knew, and he began saving his money. Eventually he had enough saved to purchase a popular video gaming system he saw on TV. I explained to him that it was his money, and he could buy the system if he wanted, but likely he would get bored playing with it in a few months and it would take him a long time to save up that much money again.

Instead, I suggested he use his money to make more money by starting a small business.

We talked about a lemonade stand, but since we live in an area with a lot of rain, it would likely not be that successful. Instead, we decided to buy a simple candy gumball machine and place it at a friend's business location, where there was plenty of foot traffic and a need to wait around for services.

After the first month in business, Lucas and I went back to the machine and collected the coins. We sat down together, and I explained how much money was actual profit—and how much of it was an expense to be repaid or reinvested into buying more gumballs. In just a few short months, Lucas had recovered enough money to pay for the gumball machine and was making a small but steady stream of income.

I explained if he still wanted to buy that video gaming system, he could. Lucas told me he had been playing it at his friend's house and I was right, he had become bored with it. Instead, he wanted to buy another gumball machine. Although I didn't know it at the time, Lucas was my first unofficial YET (Young Entrepreneur Training) Student!

By the time Lucas was fourteen, he owned over 100 gumball machines throughout the city. He started to attend some business conferences with me, where he earned the nickname, "The Gumball Kid" after sharing his story on stage. He then authored a book with the same title. (You can visit www.GumBallKid.com to purchase a copy)

He was invited to be a guest on the *Rich Dad Radio Show*, hosted by Robert Kiyosaki. At the age of sixteen, he was invited by Verne Harnish, best-selling author and owner of Gazelles, Growing Leaders—Growing Companies to speak on stage in front of 650 large business owners in Las Vegas, Nevada.

That was a life-changing day in his life. He was offered the opportunity to travel to other countries to speak and help motivate other young people. He sold more copies of his book than any other professional speaker at the two-day event. Not bad for a kid!

As Lucas began to share his story from stage, other parents and people asked me, "How did you do that?" and "Can you teach my kids?" and "Where did you learn what to teach him?" I then realized if I could teach my children, I might be able to teach other kids too. This lightbulb moment was the beginning of the Young Entrepreneur Training (YET) program . . . and this book.

It may sound like it was a lot of work to mentor Lucas, but it wasn't, and it won't be hard for you to mentor your child if you follow the steps and act on what we are about to share with you. It's actually really easy!

Chapter 7
Norma's Story

I grew up as a child of divorce. I lived with my mom. She found employment at a coffee shop close to our one-room apartment. We lived there and shared a bed until I was almost nine-years-old. At the age of eight, I came home after school one day feeling hungry. Mom was at work and I opened the fridge door. It was quite bare, but it did have a package of six hot dog wieners— and I decided to cook one. Boiling a hot dog on my own was exciting and even though I wasn't hungry, the novelty of cooking resulted in me cooking three more, all of which I promptly ate. When Mom came home, I told her about my new-found skill and independence.

My mom looked sad and afraid—not excited like I thought she would be. She explained I was not to be using the stove without supervision and those six hot dogs were destined to be our dinner until her next payday.

For the next two evenings, I ate a hot dog while my mom sipped a cup of tea. She told me she wasn't hungry, but instinctively I knew that wasn't true. I was so happy and relieved when she received her pay cheque on Friday and we could go grocery shopping. I realized during that experience, money was important in our daily life.

My mom married my stepdad when I was nine-years-old. He was a good, hardworking union man; it took four years of saving for them to make a small down payment on a simple three-bedroom home in a blue-collar community. Later that same year, my half-sister was born.

A few months later, my stepdad's union went on an eight-month strike. Their savings had been wiped out from the purchase of the house and not having a regular pay cheque put a lot of pressure on our family. It was not uncommon to hear them arguing about money. Lack of money created a lot of hardship in our home and in their relationship.

As a teen, I started to spend more time with my birth dad. He owned a small business and worked six days a week. I worked with him on Saturdays.

My birth dad did talk about money, but never in a positive way and never directly to me. I would overhear conversations he had with others. They were mostly negative, and I learned, "there was never enough money"; "people were cheap"; and, "everyone wanted something for nothing." He also talked a lot about how owning a business was more work than it was worth. For me, this was very confusing; I worked behind the sales counter and saw a lot of money come into the business, but we never had any conversations about expenses or profit.

Many kids in my neighborhood never even completed high school. For many girls, the common thought was to "find a rich husband" and if we wanted out of the neighbourhood, we had "best be looking good" if we wanted to find someone wealthy. Self-esteem was hard to come by back then. It was a community where many people lived on Social Service benefits and had little or no desire to find a job. Many worked for minimum wage or lived off the proceeds of crime. Quite frankly, there were a lot of people in my neighborhood who had drinking and drug problems.

Positive messages about money were few. Many people talked down on others they viewed as rich, and the overall feeling was, it was my destiny to be poor—or at best, lower middle class.

My parents were good people who tried their best to raise me right and give me guidance. However, they allowed me to make my own decisions about money, jobs, and my future. I was a defiant teen and quite headstrong. I worked part-time since I was fourteen and thought I had life all figured out. Crazy as this may sound, my parents even signed the paperwork that allowed me to get married before the age of consent (and I wasn't pregnant).

Just after getting married, I left my very good-paying part-time job to work full-time hours in a salaried position at an office. Regretfully, no one told me—and I was too naive to understand—I was going to work forty hours a week for the same money as my part-time job.

I looked back and thought, *Why did my parents allow me to get married so young? Why didn't anyone explain the difference between an hourly wage and a salary?* I now realize it was likely because money was tight at home and I would be one less mouth to feed. Although money was never openly discussed, I always knew there was never a lot of extra at the end of the month.

I married at the age of seventeen, gave birth to twin boys when I was eighteen and at nineteen I moved to a new city, away from my family where my husband and I bought our first home. Just before my twins were a year old, I left my husband and became a single parent.

Talk about growing up quickly! I was young, naïve, and had two babies to support. I remained strong-willed and stubborn and although I needed to use Social Service programs as a stepping-stone to get back on my own two feet, I was determined my fate in life would be better than what I had witnessed growing up.

Soon I found my own financial footing and could support my little family without help. I shared an apartment to keep costs low and I worked full-time during the day and part-time at night. Unfortunately, things fell apart for my former husband as well. Our mortgage payments were not being paid, our joint credit cards were overloaded and after leaving, I quickly ran my own credit cards to their limit. Neither one of us could feed the Money Monster we had created. Eventually our home was sold, and all equity was lost.

Even as a young mom, credit had been so easy for me to get. There was never any discussion about how hard it would be to pay back the money I borrowed. I ended up declaring personal bankruptcy, which hurt my heart more than I can ever express. I made the decision that lack of money was never going to ruin my life again. My challenge? I didn't really know how to manage money and had to figure it out for myself.

At the age of twenty-five, I met and married my forever husband, Jeff. He wanted the same things in life as I did. Within eighteen months of our marriage, we saved enough to buy our first home together.

We both instinctively knew buying rental properties was a smart thing to do, but we had no one to teach us or guide us. It took us almost nine years of saving to buy our first rental property and another year or so to buy our second one. We then stopped buying rental units for almost six years because we could not figure out how to qualify for more mortgages.

One night, while watching late night TV, Jeff saw a PBS Special with Robert Kiyosaki talking about his book *Rich Dad, Poor Dad*. He bought the book, read through it in a few evenings and then convinced me we should go to an evening presentation based on the principles of the book. This was the first step into a new way of thinking about money for both of us.

Over the years we attended many conferences and courses on real estate. We didn't buy any more rental properties, though. Our own fears about money would not allow us to take any extra risks. Eventually we were exposed to a three-day personal development training called the Millionaire Mind Intensive, which was life-changing. We learned how to revisit our money memories, accept the ones that served us well, and get rid of the ones that did not. We also learned to quiet the little voice in our head and to manage our money in a smarter way. We bought an additional thirty rental properties within the next year.

Jeff and I share a son named Levi, who had no interest in furthering his education beyond high school. Levi had attended the Millionaire Mind Intensive with us and at the age of seventeen, he asked us if we could invest his education money into real estate for him. As of the writing of this book, he is currently a partner with us in a couple of different properties and following his own entrepreneurial path.

Although I also have twin sons who are older than Levi, I don't include their financial path or development in this book because I didn't teach them about money. I didn't really learn about money until they were thirty-years-old. When they were growing up, I was like most people. Money was a taboo topic and I never had candid talks with them on the subject. This is one of my greatest regrets. The reality is, I could not teach them what I did not know.

Chapter 8
The Universe Provides Lessons

Neither one of us believes in accidental events or chance happenings. Everything that happens in life happens for a reason. Some of these things can teach us lifelong lessons—if we are willing to look for them. Although some of our past events were quite painful, they were all lessons we needed to learn. We also believe by sharing our past, we can potentially spare someone else from pain in the future.

When we first met up at a monthly entrepreneur event, Lance was raising his blended family, including his teenager Lucas, who he would bring to the meetings; and I was raising our teenage granddaughter who was the same age. We were both naturally drawn to each other and sat together on a regular basis. Over time, we started to share our backgrounds and found many commonalities. We had both read *Rich Dad Poor Dad* and we had both attended the Millionaire Mind Intensive programs, albeit at different times.

As Lance started to develop the YET program, I started to share with him my background and skill sets, and I found them to be quite complementary to what he was doing. We decided we wanted to join forces and make YET into a globally recognized program and to write and publish this book together.

What we have both learned and believe is, "The Universe is always on target" and "like energy attracts like energy." We are both positive-thinking individuals with entrepreneurial spirits. It seemed only natural to work together on this project.

If you understand and believe in the same things as we do, the next thought in your mind could be, *I guess it's not an accident I'm reading this book then*. At least we hope you are having that thought, or something similar. If you have never heard of the concept, we hope we have introduced you to a new way of thinking.

We truly believe there is a reason you are here reading this book, at this moment in time.

Collectively we have done well in life, with plans to do better and make the world a better place, one life at a time. We have learned a lot of good life lessons we can continue to build on and share with others.

Lesson # 1—Choose to Never Fail

When we say, "never fail" it does not mean we don't want you to make mistakes. Quite the contrary. We know you are going to make mistakes. We all do. It's how we learn when trying something new. Remember learning how to do basic math? Mistakes were made all the time. The key was that you learned from each mistake. You looked back at the problem, figured out what you did wrong and then corrected your error.

Choosing to never fail follows the same process. We no longer fail in life. We either win or we learn the lesson. If something in our life does not go as planned, we do not view it as a failure—it is an opportunity. It's an opportunity to learn a lesson, and once a lesson is learned, it is not to be repeated.

We hope you can take this same attitude into your life and teach it to your children. After all, no one learned to walk without falling when they were babies. Each time a baby falls, he or she figures out what to do to walk further before the next fall. Life lesson simplified.

Lesson # 2—Education Is Rarely Free But Often Priceless

Some of those life lessons have cost us a lot of money. We used to think of that as money wasted. With our new perspective, we now see the money that was lost or wasted was the price of our education. Many people go to university or college and spend a lot of money on formal education, but life lessons can be more valuable in the long run. It is the price we pay to learn by doing—or in some cases, by not doing.

When we have an experience many would see as negative, we think differently. We know when something unexpected happens to us, it is a lesson for us. For example, if you lend a friend $500 and he never pays it back, it was likely the best money you ever spent. The cost of learning the truth about someone's morals and values is priceless.

Lesson # 3—The BIG Life Lesson for a Strong Financial Future

The big life lesson we really want to share with you and the world is this: We NEED to talk openly about money with kids from an early age. The reality is, money *does* make the world go around, so let's face our own fears and start talking about money on a regular basis. If we want things to change in our world, we must be the change we want to see. It's been remarkable how quickly our kids and the YET students became interested in how money works, how to make more of it, and how to share what they are learning.

You might be nervous or reluctant to talk about a subject and not know all there is to know. It's totally OK if and when you talk about money, you admit your knowledge is limited. Admitting you don't know the answer but stating you will find out, will lead to conversations where both you and your children will learn together and establish more trust between you. If you allow your lack of confidence to start the conversation about money, neither you nor your kids will ever grow or learn.

Part 3

Chapter 9
A Kid's Perspective on Money

When you were a little kid, you likely remember seeing people with things you wanted to have. You would ask your parents for the money or ask them to buy it for you. Sometimes they would say yes, but not always.

As a kid, your wants were unlimited; you didn't have the filters of experience life will eventually provide. You didn't know money or time can limit what you can have. As a result, you didn't have any real concept of what it took or what your parents had to do, or give up, to provide the things they wanted and needed.

So, even though your parents may have said yes, or purchased something for you, you were likely to ask for more. It's not that you were greedy; you just didn't understand limits yet.

In this era, with new technology changing how we pay for things, such as online banking, debit and credit cards, and payments made through cell phones, it's really no surprise kids don't understand where money comes from or that it is in limited supply.

They see everyone from Mom and Dad and Grandma to strangers in a grocery store simply pull out a plastic card from their wallet or flash their phone at the cashier's screen. The cashier then hands over the goods purchased or provides a receipt for the meal or experience they are about to enjoy. It's no wonder kids haven't a clue. Money is often invisible.

The myth of unlimited money continues when they are taken to an ATM or into most banks. The plastic card goes into a machine—and magically cash appears.

From a kid's point of view, they just want one of those magic cash devices. They have no idea where the money comes from or how it gets there in the first place. They don't understand how money is earned and how it gets into the banking system. So how can we possibly expect them to understand each bank account has a limit, according to the person that owns it. They simply see the money come out and not go in, and this is where the problem starts.

Now, as adults we know those beliefs are simply not true. From a kid's viewpoint, we need to talk to them about where money comes from. We need to ask them, "How do you get it and how can you get more of it?"

Chapter 10

Where Does Money Come From?

You Can Receive Money as a Gift

This is a great way to get more money. Think back and you will find times in your life where money was just given to you. Perhaps it was as early and as easy as a visit from the Tooth Fairy. Do you remember opening a birthday card and finding money inside? (We both loved receiving birthday money when we were kids.) If you are lucky as an adult, you might even have received a Christmas or year-end bonus from your job that was paid out in cash. Let's not forget the one most all people dream about—winning the lottery! Even winning a few bucks on a lottery ticket is considered receiving money as a gift.

Unfortunately, as fun and exciting as it is to receive gift money, this is a money source that cannot be relied upon. We only have so many baby teeth to give to the tooth fairy and based on most people's experience, winning the lottery is not common either. No one can rely on a steady source of gift money to live on throughout their life.

You Can Work for Money

Majority of adults over the age of eighteen will work for money. They will trade their time, their skills, or their knowledge for a wage, either hourly or salaried, or on a contract basis. They will have a boss or someone they must report to, and someone else will determine how much money they will be paid, when they will work and even when they will take their holidays. They must rely on someone else's decisions to maintain their source of income.

It's perfectly OK to work for money. If you love your job, why wouldn't you work for money? Our opinion is, if your work makes you happy and you learn how to manage your money wisely, we encourage you to enjoy working. The key to staying happy as a working employee is simple—it's about having the choice to go to work every day. In fact, I (Norma) stayed at my job for six years longer than I needed to, simply because I loved my job.

Money from a Government/Charitable Program

Some people in life receive money from a government program such as Social Services, a Disability Program, or other charitable programs to help those in need. Most of these programs are not designed to be sustainable nor a long-term solution for people. The monies paid are usually contingent upon guidelines that must be adhered to and are rarely abundant in their amounts.

Most people that receive money from these programs do not have an easy life, and there is rarely extra money for the nicer things we all like to enjoy. We encourage you to have a conversation about these kinds of programs with your children. Explain to them other than disability-type programs, government programs are intended as stepping-stones to a better life, not as an ideal lifestyle. Teach your kids to be kind, non-judgemental and grateful programs are in place for those having a hard time in life.

You Can Earn Money by Becoming an Entrepreneur

Fewer people take the route of entrepreneur. However, most of the truly wealthy people in this world are business people. They create their own destiny and path. The happiest of entrepreneurs create or buy a business based around their individual interests and passions. Many of the greatest entrepreneurs we know insist they never work a day in their life, yet they put more hours into their business than a traditional work-for-money employee ever did. Entrepreneurs create an income directly in proportion to their efforts and by creating a great team of like-minded individuals to learn and grow with.

You Can Give Your Money a Job!

In our experience, this is the best way to make money. Our goal is always to have our money work harder than we do. Money can be invested to create more money. The key to giving your money a job is understanding where you are sending it to work, understanding how much risk that money might be taking, how often the money will be paid, and how much it will be paid (often called a Return on Investment, or ROI).

When you put your money to work, it is sometimes called passive income or mailbox money. A simple way to remember this is that you do not have to be active yourself to earn the money; or the money may come back to you in the form of a cheque in the mail.

This is the area where most people get confused. Don't worry if you are one of them. The point is, it is an area that can be learned about. Just remember, learn from someone who has what you want and has been where you started.

You Can Steal Money or Print Money

Clearly neither stealing nor counterfeiting money is an option you can teach your children, nor is it an option we want to suggest. It is illegal and simply the wrong way to get ahead in life. It may provide you with a short-term solution, but it will end up costing you a lifetime of regret. We will not be teaching you to steal or print money in this book—and you will not be teaching your children this option either. We do encourage you to have a conversation with your kids, though, about the right and wrong of these activities and how they negatively impact people, themselves, and the world.

Chapter 11
Managing Systems

Successful businesses follow systems. One of the most recognizable companies in the world is McDonald's, home of the Big Mac. No matter where you go in the world, their fries are all made the exact same way, a Big Mac has the same ingredients and they serve Coca Cola products as their beverages. The same could be said for Walmart, or Taco Bell, or any number of large companies. Each one of these businesses could literally take an employee from one location and place them into another and they would know exactly what to do in their job. Simply put, systems create success. Systems also create simplicity.

Successful people create and follow systems to make their lives easier and to ensure continued success. They also manage and respect their money—and it doesn't matter how much money they have. It would be rare to find a truly successful person who does not keep their money and credit cards tidy in a wallet or billfold.

It would also be extremely rare for them not to know where their investments are located and their value. Although they may employ a team of accountants and bookkeepers and other professionals to help manage their money, the bottom line is they OVERSEE their team. They don't just put their money in someone else's hands and hope it grows or is spent wisely.

While neither one of us is currently worth multimillions of dollars, we are happy, healthy, and financially comfortable. We can choose to work or not; we own businesses, and we have investments that create passive income. Our lives are on track to live each day as we like. It is rare for either of us to set an alarm clock unless an early morning flight has been booked or we decide to make an early morning appointment. In short, life is good and we live in a way that makes us each happy.

We can maintain these lifestyles because we manage our money. We control where it gets spent, when, and on what. By teaching and following a money management system, you and your children can also live a life of choice. The sooner you start to teach your children, the quicker the system becomes ingrained in them as a natural habit, just like brushing their teeth.

All parents should want to raise children to be happy, healthy, and successful in life. Can you imagine how disheartening it is to both parent and child if, as a young adult, the child returns home and says, "Mom, Dad, I need help. I didn't make the right choices and now I'm in financial trouble?"

You taught your kids to talk and walk. You teach them right from wrong. They use your teaching daily without much thought as to why they do certain things. You need to help them learn to do the same with money: use money wisely and create good habits that become second nature.

The earlier you can start to teach them responsible money management, the easier it is to set them on a good path. They will stay on path in the future because they will be developing a lifetime habit—without even thinking about it. That process starts one step at a time. We believe the first step is to provide them with the tools to learn, which means some money of their own will be required.

Chapter 12
Kids and Allowances

Have you ever tried to explain something to someone they've never done?

Take the sport of hockey as an example. You'd have to explain how to skate, how the game itself works, the different player positions, the difference between defense, offence, the rules, how penalties are called, the different kinds of penalties, such as off-side penalties, icing, sticking and so on. There are so many different aspects to the game it would take a long time to explain and understand.

As a good coach, you would advise the person you are teaching to study everything they can about hockey. With enough reading and discussion and even watching of the game, you could potentially convince them they could win the MVP (Most Valuable Player) award.

However, when the time comes for them to strap the skates on and go into the game, a whole new world appears the second they step on the ice. They fall on their butt and suddenly realize all the preparation in the world couldn't prepare them for ice being that slippery. That MVP trophy just got even further away. Then you as their coach and they as the player are both disheartened.

The same happens with money. We can tell you how to teach your kids. We can tell you and them how to manage money, and we can describe how it looks and feels to do it. We can talk about what the results will be. However, it is an entirely new experience when there is physical, cold, hard cash in hand, and your kids are doing the math and making choices about how to manage money.

If you want to learn how to play hockey, then strap some skates on and get on the ice. If you want someone to learn to manage money, then put it in their hands.

Allowances—Yes or No?

Some people do not believe in giving their children an allowance. We feel differently.

If you consciously start to add up all the things you pay out of pocket for your kids during a month, you are probably spending more than you realize. Kids without allowances are forever coming to Mom and Dad and asking for money to buy things (snacks, clothes, makeup, video games, books) and be able to do things like go to the movies or go swimming with friends.

Instead of your kids thinking of you as an instant cash machine, you could take a portion of the money you are spending on them anyway and give it to them as an allowance. You can help them by teaching them how to manage it and letting them pay for some of those things you were previously shelling out cash for.

You'll spend the same amount of money as before (perhaps even less), but you will teach them a life skill in the process. It could also teach them to appreciate you and the money you had been spending on them in the past. Learning appreciation is just a bonus.

Two Schools of Thought on Allowances

We have two different ways to look at allowances, and we're not going to tell you which one you should do. We'd like you to keep an open mind as you read through these next two chapters and then choose a method that you think will work best for your family!

Chapter 13
Allowance Money for Chores

Lots of people think kids should get an allowance but only if they earn it by doing chores. They are given a list of jobs, such as doing the dishes, cutting the grass, folding the laundry, or taking out the garbage. In return, they will be paid for their work. Makes sense, right? We all go to work and when we finish what we are supposed to do, the boss pays us.

The challenge we have seen and experienced is, you must become your children's boss. Did they do the job? Did they do it right? What if only some of the chores are done? Do they get paid if they were sick and not able to do the chores? You lose your role as parent and take on the role of employer. Rarely do people love their boss and you can't fire your children!

So, is an allowance for chores the best way to teach our kids?

This method teaches kids some work ethic and helps them become contributing members of society. They do a job and they get paid. But it often becomes a battle between parent and child—and between siblings as well. It's very difficult to assign a dollar value to each chore in a way that a child understands is fair. It's a common way of handling allowance in many homes, but in our opinion, it creates much more stress than we think it's worth.

Chapter 14

Allowance for Money Management

From Lance's home: We give each child an allowance; however, there are two rules which are attached to receiving the money, regardless of the age of the child.

First Rule:

The allowance is given with the sole purpose of learning to manage money. Although the money is given without a chore list attached, we still expect our kids to be contributing members to the household on a regular basis and help with things like dishes, feeding the cat, and laundry.

Second Rule:

To receive their allowance, they must attend the meeting we, as parents have designated as, "Allowance Hour." If a child does not attend, he or she does not get paid. No exceptions to the rule.

As parents, we designate an Allowance Hour every second week. Currently it is every second week on a Thursday night, right after dinner, because it's the one night a week where the kids are all home and not involved in an outside activity.

How Much Should Allowance Be?

Every household is going to be different. The amount of money for each child is entirely up to you. You must make sure you can afford what you give them, and it shouldn't be something that is too high or too low. You also need to make sure you can consistently pay out the allowance on a regular and on-going basis.

In our home, we have chosen to use each child's age as a guide. Our ten-year-old gets $10 every two weeks and our thirteen-year-old gets $13 every two weeks, and so on. The kids stop getting allowance when they turn nineteen. At that point, they are adults and should be set on the right path. This isn't a rule, so if you're starting your child on an allowance in their later teen years, you may want to keep going beyond the age of nineteen if it makes sense in your home. The most important part is to allow enough time to receive an allowance for money management to become an ingrained habit and one they can follow for the rest of their life.

On each child's birthday, we celebrate they will be getting a raise and the increase takes place on the next allowance day. This way everyone gets equal raises and they know when to expect them. This also eliminates any arguing between siblings.

If a younger child complains because they don't get as much as an older child, you can explain to them when the older child turns nineteen, they will no longer get an allowance—so it all adds up to the same amount of money over time.

The choice is yours; you can choose the allowance money for chores method or the allowance money for management method. The amount you give your kids for allowance is up to you, as are the outcomes that come with each choice. For us it was easy—there is no stress at our house regarding allowance, and the opportunity to talk openly about money is working well.

Chapter 15
Wants and Needs

Spending money is an everyday part of life and an important aspect of learning money management. We spend money on things we want and on things we need. When money is tight, often our wants must be moved to the bottom of the priority list until we can afford them.

So it only makes sense to start teaching kids early in life the difference between a Want and a Need. Some people may prefer to use the terms, "Must-Haves" and "Nice-to-Haves" when speaking to their children. You can choose whichever terms make the most sense to you.

We think it's important to teach kids the difference between a Need and a Want, as it is the invisible line between these two that often creates unhappy and unfulfilled people. Ultimately this can lead to excessive spending and massive bad debt when credit becomes available. It is this lack of distinction between the two that is the birth of the Money Monster mentality.

Marketing, commercials, social media, and advertising all blur the line between a need and a want to the point it has become almost invisible. On average, we are exposed to 3,000 ads per day. Advertising is impossible to avoid and is easy to recognize—from ads on TV, radio, or billboards to the less obvious product placements in TV shows and movies, logos on clothing, signs on gas station pumps, and even ads on the back of bathroom stalls.

When we were growing up, the topics of Wants versus Needs was never a discussion in either of our homes. Looking back at our spending, most of the credit card debt we incurred was for Wants—foolish things like expensive dinners out with friends, movie tickets, ski passes, concert tickets, fancy footwear, or the latest technology or toy.

Shopping and spending should not be a hobby or pastime, and yet, "hanging out at the mall" has become normalized as something to do when we are bored or as a social outing. It's important to teach our kids that shopping is something we should be doing consciously and with purpose.

You can start by setting an example for your kids. Before going shopping, share with them the list of items you intend to purchase and have a dollar value attached either to each item or to the total shopping trip.

We suggest you start with just a few items at a time. This can be as simple as shopping for a birthday gift for their friend or for a few clothing items for your child. Prepare ahead of time by showing them the list and discussing the amount of money you will be spending. During the outing, you may need to remind them when the money is gone, the trip will be finished—and you will not be returning or buying those items on a different day. This is a great way to help kids see they *need* to buy the items on the list and although they may *want* a forty-dollar T-shirt, they may have to choose a less expensive shirt to ensure they get everything that is truly needed.

Grocery shopping is another opportunity to engage them in discussion about Wants and Needs. Let them see the list of things you need to buy and set the total limit for the trip. While shopping, you can pick up impulse items such as magazines, kitchen tools, or junk food and engage your kids by asking them if it is on the list. If it's not on the list, you can explain the item was a Want, and since you have a list to follow, you will have to wait for another day to make the purchase. You are leading by example and showing your kids we can't always have what we want, when we want it.

If you view grocery shopping with kids as a painful experience, you can help them stay entertained and engaged by being active in the purchasing process with you. Tell them what is on the list (if they can't yet read) and ask them to help you by spotting the items. If there is a variety of price points for the item you are purchasing, you can explain why you are buying the one you chose. It may be based on quality of the product or on the volume you get for the money; for example, it's often cheaper to buy a big box of corn flakes than a small one if you are comparing quantity).

If they can read, ask your child to tick off the items on your list as you fill the cart. You can pick up an item and ask them if it belongs in the cart or not. Ask them to identify it as a Need or Want item and then put the Want items back on the shelf. Help them see managing your money by prioritizing shopping items based on Want and Need is important by showing them you can resist an impulse purchase. Remember, kids learn by what they see us do, not by what we tell them to do!

Another opportunity to share with your children is larger purchases. For example, if you are planning to buy a new washer and dryer set because you have renovated the laundry room, but still have working appliances, ask your child if they think it is a Want or Need purchase. There is nothing wrong with buying Wants if you can afford the item and are not purchasing it on credit. Ask them if the old appliances were broken, would the new ones then be a Want or a Need? You could even further the discussion by showing them appliances in different price ranges, discussing the Want features versus the Need features and asking them which ones they think you should purchase based on the reason you are replacing them.

As your kids start school and become more socially aware and influenced by their peers, shopping for Wants and Needs will become a larger and more complicated discussion and process. However, since shopping requires money, it is a necessary discussion.

Money management and shopping for value as well as making purchases for tweens, teens, and young adults is really a double challenge. At this age they start to understand the difference between a Want and a Need; however, they also need to feel good about themselves and fitting in to their social circle is often determined by owning or wearing the right clothing or owning the latest gadget.

Sometimes the item the kids Want is also a Need. It's the need to fit in. Unfortunately, advertising and marketing puts a lot of pressure on our kids (heck, on adults too). Most people want to fit in, feel comfortable in a group and not stand out as unique or different. We want to feel confident in ourselves and look good at the same time. The line between Wants and Needs becomes very blurry!

For example, a winter coat is a Need, but the value you can spend on the coat can range wildly in price, not just for quality, but because of branding and marketing. Does your child *need* to spend $200 on a brand-name coat or do they *want* that particular coat to fit in? A $75 coat would likely fill the physical Need, but not the emotional one.

It's a lot easier to start talking to your kids way before the emotional confusion of Wants and Needs become apparent. You can start this conversation when they are around six- to eight-years-old, depending on their maturity level. The following types of discussions can help them make decisions later when they may feel the pressure to own something others have.

Ask your kids how they feel when they see other kids with stuff they see on TV or in the stores. Does not owning that item make them feel anxious or left out? Do they think people would like them more if they owned that item? How do they choose their friends? Do they choose them based on what they wear, what they own, or because they have similar interests and are nice kids?

Marketing is designed to turn us into consumers, not wise shoppers. Talking openly about advertising and how it manipulates our emotions is the first step in helping your kids understand the difference between a Want and a Need when it comes to shopping for stuff that will impact their self-confidence.

You can talk to them about commercials on TV, billboards along the road, or ads in a magazine. Encourage smart shopping by talking about what the advertisers are trying to sell. Do they really think they will skate faster or jump higher if they eat a particular type of cereal or wear a popular brand name shirt or shoes? You can point out and discuss how some product packaging and their pictures are designed to make a product more appealing and yet may not provide the benefits the pictures indicate it might.

Whether you are aware of it or not, you are teaching your children about money every time you go shopping. Teaching your kids how to become smart shoppers is as simple as looking at your own spending and considering whether you are teaching them good habits or bad ones. You may need to alter some of your habits or leave your kids at home on the days you know your, "bad habits" are likely to be observed!

It is not the items purchased that are important—it is the discussion you create with your kids. Let them know it is OK to have Wants and make a Want purchase. What is critical is, Want purchases are well thought out, not bought on an impulse and provides good value to the buyer. It is also vital to help them learn how to plan for items in the Want category. The good news we can share with you is, this is part of our Money Master system and will be coming up in the next chapter!

Part 4

Chapter 16

Money Master Management—Mmm...

Everyone Loves a Good Thing That Makes Life Sweeter!

We are hoping we have now whetted your appetite enough to be ready to bite into the "Sweet Spot" of the "Mmm" and have decided on the best allowance system for your family. After all, if the kids don't have any money to manage, how would they be able to put into practise what you are about to teach them?

In the next chapters, we will cover the different categories in the system; exactly what an "Allowance Hour" can look like and even a little on how to put some of your personal finances into a system that works for you too! We won't go into a lot of adult info YET, as there might be another book in our future. Get it? Sorry, bad joke—we're just excited about the YET program for kids.

Six Categories in the Mmm

There are six categories all net income or money from any source needs to be allocated.

Necessities of Life

Save to Spend

Education

Play

Wealth

Give

For ease of reading, we are going to refer to each category by its name and use the term *jar* as the place the money would be placed. This makes sense for kids—they love to see their money grow, and they are usually visual learners. Quite frankly, so are some adults. We are hoping as a parent, you will lead by example and consider using the system, or a modified part of the system, as well.

As an adult, you could choose to use a series of bank accounts if that makes more sense to you or start off with using jars or envelopes. Later in the book we will delve more into how using online banking and the Mmm system can work for you!

We use percentages to share how much money is to be allocated in each area and if you are an adult currently struggling with debt or simply new to money management, we don't want you to panic. We will address how you can adjust the system for your personal circumstances later in the book.

Beside each jar heading, we have placed two percentages: The first will be for kids fifteen and under (as we presume they do not yet have any necessities of life expenses and no bad debt); the second percentage is for kids sixteen and over, including adults.

Allowance Hour

Earlier in the book we discussed the need to give your kids an allowance, so they have actual cash in their hands. No matter which method for allowance your family decided upon, there is an additional step in making the Money Master Management (Mmm) system a part of their lives.

That step is setting up a time to provide the money to the kids and have money discussions. We call this time the "Allowance Hour," although it may not take that much time in your home. The purpose of this time is for your kids to receive the allowance and to create an opportunity to talk about money. As you go through this book, you will find different lists and ideas to help make this time both enjoyable and fun for all of you, and later a full chapter will be devoted to this topic.

A Young Adult's Perspective

My name is Lucas Dinahan, and I'm the one they nicknamed, "The Gumball Kid" when I was fourteen-years-old. Lance is my dad, and I guess you could say I was his first YET student, even though the program hadn't been developed or even conceived as an idea. As earlier chapters indicate, I had the opportunity to hang out with my dad and grow up learning about what is now called the Money Master Management (Mmm) Jar System.

As of the writing of this book, I'm nineteen-years-old, and I sold my candy vending business a few years back. Now I work full time as an apprentice electrician, and I am learning and running a stock market trading account using the money in my Wealth Jar.

Looking back, I learned the most when I was running my vending machine business. I started out with one machine and ended up with almost four hundred. Pretty good growth, I think, for a kid's business. The money basics I learned from my dad and by running my business are the habits I use today.

I use the Mmm system, but I use a series of bank accounts instead of the jars. My pay cheque is direct-deposited to my main chequing account, and I consider that account as my Necessities of Life Jar. Fifty-five percent of my cheque stays there to cover things I must pay for on a regular basis. I then transfer the remaining 45% of my paycheque into the other accounts using online banking.

If I want to make a purchase that should be coming from any of my other accounts including the Education, Play, Save to Spend Savings, Wealth, my stock trading account, or my Donation Jars, I simply use my debit card to pay for the item from my Necessities of Life chequing account and then transfer that same amount from the account it belongs to back into my main chequing.

I really like using the Mmm system online. It's a good visual when I sign in online via my phone, and I can see where all my money is and how I have allocated money to the different areas. I like that at the bottom of my screen I can see the total amount of all accounts combined. It's a mass of money, all in one place, but it's divided so I can spend with confidence on the things that matter most.

I can easily identify if my future needs (like new tires for my car) are being planned for and quickly see how much I have saved up in the Save to Spend/Short-Term Savings account to make sure I'll be prepared when I need to make that purchase. Having my money managed with the different jar categories means that I don't spend my money in stupid ways. I really think about what I am buying and the effect it will have on my life. I think I make better decisions overall, and it feels good to manage my money.

I recently got my first credit card, and it's very interesting. It's so tempting to buy stuff, but it's not even money I've earned yet. It's way too easy to overspend. I almost maxed the card out in the first month, because I didn't keep track of exactly how much I had charged on the card. I've been taught that to avoid interest charges I have to pay it off as soon as the statement arrives.

I hated the feeling of not knowing exactly how much I had spent on the credit card, but knowing I was supposed to pay it off in full. I spent money that was essentially invisible until I received the credit card statement—and then the money became very real. The credit limit gets reached so fast; it was shocking how quickly everything added up. My dad warned me that it was going to take some real attention not to get into debt, and he was right. I'm a lot more cautious about using it now.

I'm happy that I was lucky enough to have a dad that cared enough to teach me all the stuff he did. I have a better handle on managing and spending my money than most of the guys my age. Some of my friends do better with managing their money than others, but I feel like I have a much better grasp than the majority.

Most of my friends live paycheque-to-paycheque. They get paid, and two weeks later they are broke. One of them doesn't even plan to pay for his necessities like rent first. He buys clothes, shoes, and electronics, eats out a lot, and spends a lot of money on partying. He does that with his entire first paycheque of the month and then scrambles to have enough money to pay for his rent and buy food with the second paycheque. He's only two weeks away from disaster if he ever lost his job or got hurt at work. He doesn't have any savings at all.

Another one of my friends burns through money like that every week; he doesn't even have a car, but he buys stupid stuff all the time. I tried to tell him he doesn't need to spend $300 on shoes, and that's why he is always bumming a ride. I get tired of that, and often now I tell him to walk to the party in his new shoes instead of allowing him to bum a ride from me.

It always blows me away how they can get a $1,000 paycheque on a Friday night, and by the following Wednesday, they are completely broke. I try to explain to my friends that money management is simple. A lot of them live at home and really don't have expenses, and yet they can't seem to understand that if they would just take 20 percent off the top of their paycheque and stick it in a separate bank account, they could buy a car or have their own place within a short period of time.

I know that I still have a lot to learn, but compared to them, I consider myself a Money Master. They are being financially eaten alive by the Money Monster. I try to give guidance to the guys I hang out with who were never exposed to stuff I learned while growing up, but the majority just want to live in the moment. I feel sorry for them. Their life is going to be hard if their work situation ever changes.

I'm not sure what my long-term future will bring. I'll always have an interest in money and putting it to work for me. My short-term goal is to see more growth in my stock trading business, but I'll likely invest in some real estate as well. My dad and I talk about money and investment opportunities on a regular basis; right now, we are looking at partnering up and investing in a mobile home park. I appreciate that we can talk about things so easily.

If you are reading this section and thinking that using this system is hard, I can tell you this. It's much easier than it sounds—and having control over my money and what I do with it is a fantastic feeling.

The YET Kids' and Passive Income

As mentioned earlier in the book, Lance tested his YET program on a group of kids. He later taught these same kids the money management system. After all, he couldn't send them into the real world knowing that without these skills the Money Monster was sure to find them.

He explained to the kids the different ways to create passive income. One of the ways to create passive income is to do something once and then be paid repeatedly for the time spent. A recording artist is an example. A recording artist will create a beautiful song and then get paid a bit of money every time it is played on the radio or downloaded from the Internet.

To help them better understand the concept, Lance offered the kids the opportunity to share their experiences with the Mmm program here in this book. Every time this book is sold, each of the kids would be paid for the time they spent with us. They were all excited about the concept—and we can tell you they will be much more excited when they start to receive royalty cheques in the future!

Throughout the next section of this book, you will find candid comments from each of the kids about the different categories of money management. We are hoping their thoughts and experiences will make it easier for you to stay motivated to teach your kids and provide some insights as to how your kids might receive the information you are going to share with them.

Chapter 17
Necessities of Life Jar (Kids 0%/Adults 55%)

In the real world, money must be used to pay for a variety of things that are truly necessities of life. Many of these expenses are things we may not want to spend our money on, but we know we need to. Things in this category include mortgage or rent payments, the phone, light, gas or water bills, insurance, car payments, gas for the car or other transportation needs, and groceries. Unfortunately, as adults, Necessities of Life is the largest portion of our income.

We talk with our young kids about Necessities of Life in general terms, as it doesn't hurt them to at least understand what they are and recognize them, but we don't expect them to contribute to them.

For kids aged sixteen and over, we start having them use this category for personal necessities like shampoo, deodorant, and makeup. You may also want to include things like their cell phone bill, gas for the car, insurance, or new tires (or at least a portion of these costs), depending on the weekly allowance they receive.

Once they get a full-time job, if they are still living at home, you may want to require them to use this category as though they were living in the real world—including charging them rent—which you can then opt to put aside to assist in their transition to their first apartment or home. After all, as parents, it should be our goal to have kids grow up and become financially independent.

Chapter 18
Save to Spend Jar
(Kids 25%/Adults 10%)

As the real world has taught us already, even with a steady paycheque we don't always have enough money to buy everything we want on payday. The same is true for kids when they get an allowance. Earlier in the book we talked about Wants and Needs. The Save to Spend Jar is for planned spending and is designed to have money set aside so when a Want is identified, the money is already in place.

    The benefit to learning and using the Save to Spend Jar is that it is designed to help buy some of the bigger, more expensive things in life. This teaches our kids that anyone can set a goal of something they want in the future—and reach the goal! It simply is a system of saving toward whatever it is you want without sacrificing the needs you must fill on a day-to-day basis.

The younger kids may use this category area of their managed money to save for a new cell phone, some Legos, a new bike, or even a Barbie doll. As the kids get older, their goals may change; they might save up for a newer car or a vacation trip with friends. As an adult, it could be a bathroom renovation, a family vacation, or even a new boat.

The point of this category is not what a person chooses to save for—it is having money earmarked and available over time for anything they want.

This jar helps to teach us although we can't always have what we want, when we want it, it's best to put a little aside each time we earn money, so it accumulates until we have enough for what we want. You may even find in the process of saving for something, its importance may change and something new might take its place. There is nothing wrong with that, but the process still needs to happen.

There are times when what you want may go on sale or the time you wanted the item may come sooner than you expected. This is a test for sure. When we don't follow a money management system and make the purchase by using a credit card, taking out a loan, or using a line of credit, the price we pay is often exponentially higher than it would have been had we waited until the money in the Save to Spend jar was available.

Unfortunately, most people do not have self-control and use credit even when they know they cannot afford to pay it off quickly. The reason credit is so readily available is, the banks and credit card companies make more money on issuing credit than they do in any other traditional lending area.

Interest rates and fees add up quickly—and many people pay for months or years after the item they purchased has long ago found its way to the recycling bin or garbage pile.

Some people justify the early purchase on credit, believing they are saving money because the item is on sale. This is rarely true. If you don't pay it off before the interest starts to accrue, you end up paying substantially more than if you had saved enough money to purchase the item at full price.

Furniture stores are famous for offering sales that are advertised as, "No Money Down, Interest-FREE for Twenty-Four Months." Sadly, if you do not pay for the furniture purchased on or before the twenty-four-month period has ended, they send you a bill with two years' worth of interest that has accrued. So the living room sofa set that was regularly priced at $2,000 and on sale for just $999 gets invoiced back to you at a rate of 28.9% interest, compounded from Day One and you now owe over $3300. Sadly, the interest on the account is going to climb higher and faster every month you carry a balance. Likely the appeal of that brand-new sofa set has worn off and the sofa set no longer looks and feels brand new either.

There are other times when the item purchased on credit has broken or outlived its usefulness long before the cost of the item plus interest has been paid off. It's not only a terrible decision—it's very frustrating to be paying down debt on an item that is no longer useable.

Buying on sale only saves you money if you have the cash to spend when it's on sale, not if you must borrow it from tomorrow's money to own it today.

The best part about waiting until you have enough in your Save to Spend Jar is the experience of pride of ownership. When you manage your money and can pay in cash, there is no guilt. You saved for this; you get to enjoy it, you earned it and no one can take that sense of pride away.

The YET Kids' Perspectives on the Save to Spend Jar

Kamryn, Age Ten

"I thought the Save to Spend Jar was never going to be used on something big, but . . . now I think it's at least my third most-used jar I have. I've used it on a lot of things I had always wanted to

buy. One of my favorite purchases was for my hamster— I got to buy her a cage and habitat for her to live and play in."

Kai, Age Thirteen

"I wasn't too sure what 'Save to Spend' meant. It was an odd name, and I was confused. Now I understand that I can save up my money in that jar to buy anything I want, and I don't have to ask my mom and dad for the money.

"Before I learned about the Jar System, I would just spend my money without thinking about things. I wasted a lot of it at dollar-type stores on stuff that broke easily. I like the Save to Spend Jar now. I really enjoy buying things that help me learn and think, things that are fun for me. Some of the puzzles I like to buy cost between $25 and $45, and now I know that I can buy them whenever I want, as long as money is in the Save to Spend Jar—and I don't have to ask permission or for money from my mom and dad."

Taya, Age Eleven

"I had no clue what that jar was when I first heard about it! Now I think it is one of my favorite jars. I use it to put money toward the things I want the most. Right now I'm saving up to buy a MacBook laptop. In our family, the rule is that if we save up for something big, like a laptop, my parents will pay half—but then my parents also get the right to use whatever we buy. I've already saved up my share, but I decided I would rather keep on saving until I have enough to buy it all by myself, so I can use it whenever I want. It will be all mine. I feel pretty good about that!"

Shaqala, Age Fifteen

"All I could see was the word SPEND on the Save to Spend Jar. It didn't take me long to see that it could help me manage my money and save for something that was a bit more expensive that I wanted, and it wasn't a jar designed to spend, spend, spend. My favorite thing I have *purchased so far is my hoverboard. Thanks to the Mmm and Jar System, I learned how to look for things that bring good value. I could buy my board privately from someone, and instead of having to spend $600 to $1,000, I was able to buy mine for just $200 because I had the money ready when the person was selling. I like this jar; it helps me think about what I want before I spend my money on just anything, and I always have money ready when I find a good deal."*

Chapter 19
Education Jar
(Kids 20%/Adults 10%)

When most people think of this category, they have one of three initial responses. The first is, "I've already completed my education" or "I have no interest in going back to school." The second thought is, "I don't have kids, so I don't need to worry about this category" or, "I don't expect my kids to pay for their own schooling." These responses are common, but we want to challenge you to think differently.

As we have learned through personal experience and from our mentors, on this earth all living things are either growing or they are dying. Those are the only two options. This is true for plants, fish, animals—and human beings. When we stop growing and learning new things, it is the beginning of the downhill slide to the other side of life, not a place any of us are in a hurry to reach.

In our opinion, "education" doesn't mean, "college or university." It means learning from other intelligent and talented people.

The Education Jar is not just for formal education. The money in this area can be used for any variety of things. It might be something simple such as a book, a course, or a seminar. Perhaps you want to learn a new skill, trade, learn to swim, paint, or even learn how to fly a plane. It doesn't matter what you are learning if you become a lifelong learner.

When we continue to use our minds to learn something new, we feel a sense of accomplishment. Growing and learning make us better people. So let's encourage it. The more you learn, the more you can grow as a person, the longer your mind will stay sharp and the healthier you'll be.

If you look carefully, you'll see that the word *earn* is imbedded in the word *learn*. We don't think that's an accident. We both take learning seriously and as a result our earning power has increased substantially, as has our zest for life. The more we learn, the more fun we have. We are constantly learning new skills and expanding our knowledge, and it is through learning that we create more free time to live life as we wish and create more money which gives us the opportunity to give back more to others. We hope from this point forward, whenever you see the word *learn*, you will remember this little story and be open to learning new things too!

We've mentioned books as one of the things you can purchase for learning, but would a comic book count? If you are already a strong reader, we would be inclined to say the answer is no. However, if you were a weak or beginning reader and the comic book would help to advance your reading ability, then a comic book could be justified.

As an adult, if you are truly committed to changing your financial picture, you could double up and get more, "bang for your buck."

You could buy something that teaches you more about your business or increases your financial knowledge and if you have a business or are an entrepreneur, it becomes a tax write-off too!

Education Jar for Kids

It's vital to help younger people see the value in continuous learning. Once again, this lifelong habit is important to instill in them while they are young and impressionable. Adults who never see the value in additional education often become couch potatoes with square eyes and fat bellies from watching too much TV. That's likely not what you want for your kids. Examples of where they could use their Education Jar money for learning might be swimming lessons, dance lessons, hockey school, computer classes, summer camps where they learn new skills or ideas, or classes where they'll learn to sing, or quilt, or play a musical instrument. All qualify as ways kids can spend money from this jar.

The best thing about the Education Jar is finding something of interest and realizing because you've managed your money, you already have the money to pay for it. You can get excited and be happy to take that class or go to that conference.

The YET Kids' Perspectives on the Education Jar

Kamryn, Age Ten

"I thought it was a good jar and it would always be empty. I need to use it for my education. So far, I haven't found too many things I wanted to spend it on. I have spent money on a course, and the course made me smarter at business."

Kai, Age Thirteen

"The name explained the jar. I like it. I haven't used any of the money yet, but I know that when I find something I want to learn about, the money will be there, and that's good."

Taya, Age Eleven

"I knew what this jar was for right from the start. You spend it on things for your education. Just your education. I've used the money in this jar to attend a different kind of learning program for kids, but when I went there, I had already learned almost everything they were teaching because I had already finished the YET program. I did learn one new thing, though, so the money was well spent."

Shaqala, Age Fifteen

"I thought the education jar was a waste of time because my parents could pay for all of my education. Now I see that my parents don't have to pay for everything, and I can pay for most of my own education. I use it now to go on school field trips and buy school supplies. I paid for my own text book fees this year. I haven't taken any extra education courses for my photography business, but that's what I'm planning to do in the future."

Chapter 20
Play Jar
(Kids 25%/Adults 10%)

This jar is everyone's favorite. Not just for kids, but for adults too, it's important in life to have some FUN. Life can't be all work, work, work and bills, bills, and bills!

If you don't get to buy something or do something fun, then what's the point of working at all? The Play Jar allows for just that. The money you save here is to spend on whatever you want. There are no rules.

Perhaps you want to spend it on some candy or a great bottle of wine, a wildly expensive dinner in a fancy restaurant, a new motorcycle, or a weekend away. You could even spend your Play Jar money on buying live worms from a fishing store and releasing them back into the earth to live a long and dirty life. It's up to you. But whatever you spend your Play Jar money on, you must enjoy doing it.

Knowing you saved the money for you to have fun and do something that makes you smile is the entire point of this category. You can spend it on a tattoo or spend it on a present for someone else. The best part of this Play Jar is knowing by using the Mmm, you can spend this money and it will fill up again, and you can have fun over and over again.

We strongly suggest you use this money to have fun on a regular basis. Make sure you spend it within thirty to sixty days; it is not intended to accumulate for a long period of time. This isn't your Planned Saving jar—it's your PLAY money!

You will find a sense of excitement and anticipation, knowing more money will be available so you can again do something fun. Happiness and fun are not always easy to find time and money for, so make sure you don't ignore this vital part of money management.

The Lego Story

One of our blended family members, Nicholas, who was eight-years-old, had been saving in his Save to Spend Jar to buy a big set of Legos he wanted for a long time. Whenever we would go shopping, he would check the prices in different stores to find the best price. As his Save to Spend Jar grew larger and larger, he became more excited about his impending purchase.

While out with his mom, he found the Lego set on sale and he believed he had finally saved enough money to make the purchase. He was very excited! His excitement soon passed when he learned he didn't have enough money after all, as he had not yet learned about tax. He came home very disappointed.

A few nights later at Allowance Hour, his experience was talked about around the kitchen table.

There was general agreement among all the kids they didn't like the idea of being taxed, but it was necessary to pay for the things they did like, such as swimming pools, schools, and nice parks to play in.

As parents we weren't surprised at their feelings, and we acknowledged it wasn't our favorite thing to spend money on either, but it was an essential part of living in society.

Nicholas was very thoughtful throughout our discussion. He really wanted that Lego set. As the discussion came around to the category of Play, a lightbulb came on for him.

He said, "If I can spend my Play money on anything I want that makes me happy, then I want to spend it on the tax, so I can buy the Lego set I want."

We had to agree, he had a valid point— so off to the store we went to buy the Lego set.

We had never seen or heard of anyone spending money on tax to be happy, but the day had come—and it came with a great big smile!

Moral of the Story: Be like Nick—Enjoy spending your Play money on things that make you happy!

The YET Kids' Perspectives on the Play Jar

Kamryn, Age Ten

"I thought it would be the Jar that I would use the most but . . . nope. It's definitely an amazing jar for me. I have used the money on a colouring book once that amused me a lot. I've used it to buy paint and crafts. When I go to the mall, I use it on clothes. Not really my favorite jar like I thought it would be—I like having the money so I can do what I want, though. It's good for that."

Kai, Age Thirteen

"I thought it was a jar where I could spend money on anything I wanted, and that's true. I like the Play Jar because I can do whatever I want with it. I used to quickly spend all my money at the dollar-type stores because I didn't have the habit of saving for what I wanted, and I wasted a lot of money. Now I know that I can have money to play with and spend on anything that makes me happy. I can even choose to put some of my play money into a different jar if it makes me happy. Sometimes I put some of it into my Save Forever Jar (Wealth Jar), because it makes me happy to know that I can get whatever I am saving for faster. Once I used the money to make a $3 bet with another kid that he wouldn't eat a piece of dog food. He ate it! I paid him the $3, and it made me laugh—I got good value for that $3."

Taya, Age Eleven

"When I first heard about the Play Jar, I thought I would use the money all in one day whenever we were paid our allowance. Now that I make my own money from my business and get allowance, I manage it better than I thought I would. Now I save and spend, save and spend, save and spend. I've used that money for lots of things, all of which made me happy at the time.

It feels good to spend it because I know I will get more money later to spend when I want on what I want."

Shaqala, Age Fifteen

"I thought whenever I had money in that jar, I would just spend it all on anything I could every week. But now I have money in there all the time, and I usually only spend it on things like chocolate or something else I have a craving for. Sometimes I buy clothes. I buy whatever I like that makes me happy in the moment."

Chapter 21
Wealth Jar
(Kids 25%/Adults 10%)

What is wealth? Wealth means different things to different people all over the world. One definition we like to use is, wealth is all about choice. Wealth is the choice and opportunity to live your life as you like, without restriction. Money or lack of money is usually what dictates how someone must live. Money in the Wealth Jar is meant to grow over time—so you can have a life of choice.

Do you remember back in Chapter 10 when we mentioned there were different ways to get money? The best way in our experience is to have money work harder for you than you do for it. The Wealth Jar is where that process starts.

Wealth money does not mean you don't do anything with the money. We don't want you to lock it away in a safe, stuff it in the mattress, or put it under a rug forever. Quite frankly, putting money away and not putting it to work is silly. A loaf of bread today is only going to get more expensive in the future, so having your money stagnant and not growing does not make sense for the long term.

There are only two rules when it comes to the Wealth Jar. That's it—two simple rules.

1. **You may only ever spend your money on something that will make you more money.**
2. **You must return any withdrawals made from your Wealth money back into the Wealth Jar once you make a profit.**

The Second Rule Is the Most Important, So We Are Going to Repeat It.

Every penny you take from your Wealth money to create more money must be returned to the Wealth Jar; the balance of the money you made will get managed back into all the jars. Your Wealth Jar should always be growing!

Kids are meant to use their Wealth Jar to create more money. They could buy what's needed to make lemonade and sell it on a hot day; they could buy supplies to make and sell cookies; they could create craft kits to sell at a farmer's market or even resell bottles of ice-cold water at a baseball diamond to parents watching the game in the stands. The ideas are endless for kid businesses. With some adult help, they could even purchase a gumball machine like Lucas did and start a business selling gumballs. Below is a list of the top ten business ideas for kids—and if you want even more ideas, you can visit our website at www.YetTraining.com and download the Top 100 Business Ideas For Kids for free.

TOP Ten Business Ideas for Kids

1. **Lemonade Stand**
2. **Lawn Mowing or Snow Shovelling**
3. **Babysitting**
4. **Dog Walking**
5. **Paper Route or Flyer Delivery**

6. Tutoring
7. Gardening
8. Running Errands for Others
9. House Sitting or Pet Sitting
10. Creating and Selling Crafts

Adults are meant to use their Wealth Jar to create more money too!

As a capable adult, you could use your Wealth Jar money to purchase a car that needs a bit of fixing up or is undervalued. You could do the work required, market the car, and sell it for more than it cost you to buy and repair.

If you had the skills, you could create a product (woodworking, sewing, knitting, or painting, for example); you could use your Wealth Jar money to purchase the raw materials and then sell the finished product to others at a profit.

You could use the money for a down payment on a rental property, as long as that house would rent for more money than it would take you to pay all the bills associated with a rental, including some long-term maintenance. In our world, we call that a positive cash-flowing property.

If you can use the money in your Wealth Jar to help you legitimately make more money, you can use that money without guilt to create a better future for yourself.

For clarity, we will use the following example to help you and your child understand exactly how the Wealth Jar works.

Lyle's Lemonade Stand

Lyle removed $10 from his Wealth Jar to buy supplies to make and sell lemonade. He had a great day of sales and at the end of the day, he ran out of lemonade and had $25 in cash.

Lyle must put back the $10 he started with from the Wealth Jar and then he must manage the $15 that's left over. Since Lyle follows the Mmm system, all his Jars will grow, including his Wealth Jar. He can repeat the process over and over. Each time he makes a profit, his Play Jar, Education Jar, Donation Jar,

Save to Spend Jar, and Wealth Jar will grow. The process can be repeated as often as he wants to run a lemonade business. Eventually Lyle will be ready to start a new kind of business and the money in his Wealth Jar will be re-purposed to support that new venture.

What Happens if the Lemonade Stand Does Not Make Money?

There are times when we take money out of our Wealth Jar with the idea of making money, but things don't work out. Perhaps the lemonade stand was on the wrong corner, or there was a fair down the road giving it away for free, or our lemonade didn't taste all that good. Then what?

What if Lyle had spent $10 and only sold $3 worth of product? Not all businesses, investments, or choices we make will make us money. Sometimes things we didn't expect or account for will happen.

At the end of the day, Lyle would have to put the $3 back into the Wealth Jar. In this example, his Wealth Jar would be less than he started with. This is not what he wanted to happen! Lyle would have lost $7 and will feel sad.

What happens if Lyle didn't make *any* money? Perhaps he tripped and spilled all the lemonade and had nothing to sell? He spent $10 and didn't even have a chance to make money. In life, sometimes things happen that we don't plan for. If something similar happened to you and all your money was lost, the process we want you to follow is the same.

Don't Lose the Lesson!

Back in Chapter 8 we referred to "Lesson #1 – Choose to Never Fail". Following is the process we want you to use to really understand what we are saying, and to teach your children.

We suggest you get a notebook with pages you cannot tear out. Take some time and think about what went wrong and why—and then sit down and write it out. If it is your child who had the experience, you may need to help him or her with this process.

Ask these kinds of questions: What went wrong? What did you not think about that caused you to lose money? What could you do differently to make sure those things will never happen again?

You may have lost $7, but that is the price of learning a lesson. Accept what has happened and learn from it. Try to never make that mistake again. Mistakes will happen, but always learn from them. If you learn from your mistake, it is no longer a mistake—it is a life lesson, one that is of value for your future. Writing something down and then reviewing it later is a great way to learn.

The reason we ask you to sit down and write things out is, it forces you to really think about all the factors that came into play as to why things didn't work out. It also helps you to see where you can do things differently in the future; it works as a source of knowledge you can go back to later and protect yourself from making a similar mistake.

The YET Kids' Perspectives on the Wealth Jar

Kamryn, Age Ten

"I thought, how could I use the money if you are not allowed to take money out? (Authors Note: The jar used to be called Save Forever). Now I see that it is one of the most important jars and one of my favorite jars—because it makes me money that I can put into my other jars. I used my money to buy supplies to make a product that I sold, and it made me a LOT more money, and then I managed the profits into my other money jars."

Kai, Age Thirteen

"When I first heard about it, I thought I would save it for something big, like a bike. Now I understand the money is to be used to save up *for things that can help me make more money. My first business was making homemade healthy dog treats. I used the money from my Wealth Jar to buy the supplies. I didn't really love that business—it was very tiring, and the dog treats were perishable so if I didn't sell them all at one time, I had to freeze them, and then the quality wasn't as good. I learned some good lessons, though. I made less treats at one time, and although I made good money from that business, I've learned to explore other business ideas, too.*

I watch a lot of YouTube videos on how to make things, and I decided I would make a special gadget designed to help fidgety people (like me). You know—people that constantly are tapping their pens on the desk, or doing other things that calm them but might annoy others around them? That kind of fidgeting. I named it a Fidgie Spinner. My design is unique in that it allows people to fidget quietly. People seem to like it a lot; I have already sold quite a few at a price of $20 each, and I expect to sell many more.

Right now, I'm saving up for a 3D printer, which will cost around $2,500. Currently I must have some of the parts for my spinner made by an outside business, but when I get my 3D printer, I can make them myself and save money on costs, which means I'll make more money on each one I sell.

I like the Wealth Jar now. It's a cool idea, and I like knowing that I will always have money to grow my business and future."

Taya, Age Eleven

"When we first started the YET program, the Jar was named differently; it was called the Save Forever Jar. I had no clue what that jar was! I thought you had to save it forever. I was confused. Now it is called the Wealth Jar, and I really like it. I spend it on stuff that will make me more money. I used the money in my Wealth Jar to buy supplies to start my first business. I bought coffee mugs and simple dishes that I could paint designs on, knowing that I could then sell them for more money. I made a LOT of money at my first selling event. I put the money I used back into my Wealth Jar, and then managed the rest into all the other jars we use. It's really great to have money to use to make more money!"

Shaqala, Age Fifteen

"This jar has become my favorite. I always thought it was a cool idea, and I still feel the same way. I bought more camera equipment, so I could take more photos, and I have also sold a lot more photos because the pictures are better quality. The money I spend from this jar helps me make more money and helps me to grow my business."

Chapter 22
Give Jar
(Kids 5% and Adults 5%)

Disclaimer: We know the percentage of 5% may not sit well with some people based on their cultural or religious belief system. It is what works for us and our families. If you would like to increase your Give Jar to a higher percentage, please take it from your Necessities of Life Jar. In most cases, you will find what you want or need in life will come from one of the other categories in the Mmm, and by using the system as we have presented it, your life will become more balanced. You will learn to live within these means and you will do very well.

There is a saying in life, it is better to give than to receive. As a young person, or even an adult who is struggling with money, this expression may not make sense. When we have very little to give, we normally resist the idea of giving it away. It's so very important to give in life and we will share our ideas with you in a minute.

We believe money attracts money and debt attracts debt. The good news is we have also experienced that giving attracts giving. The more we give, the more we receive—which means someone else is giving back! It might not be dollar for dollar or event for event, but both of our lives keep getting better. When we least expect something, something wonderful shows up in our lives. Some people refer to this as good karma.

The purpose of the Give Jar is not to give with the expectation to receive back; it is simply the bonus of making the world a better place. When you learn to give without expectation, you automatically get something back—it's called a good feeling! Knowing you can make a difference in someone's day is such a wonderful way to feel good about your life.

We want your kids to learn to manage their money including giving of money.

However, there are so many other ways you can teach them about giving as well!

You can teach them to donate their time to a good cause. Perhaps it is in cleaning up the playground or volunteering their time at a local senior home or animal shelter.

They could also be a part of helping your family giving by donating items such as old towels, pillow and blankets to a pet rescue facility. They could donate toys that are clean and in good condition to a daycare center or charity. Clothing that has been outgrown and is still in great condition can be donated to local charities or simply another family in need.

As an adult, if you are truly cash-strapped and simply cannot yet afford 5% to put into your Give Jar, we offer you another option, the option of giving your time. Time is often just as important to charities as money. Calculate the value of what 5% of your income would have been to place in the Give Jar. For example: If you would normally take home a cheque for $1200 every two weeks, 5% of that would equal

$60. Divide $60 by your hourly wage before deductions—for example, $20—and you will find you could donate three hours of your time every two weeks to a worthwhile cause in your own community.

If you choose to donate time, write down the number of hours, where you donated your time, and how it made you feel to be of service to others. Put it in the jar. Good karma attracts good karma . . . and soon you will start to see more positivity coming into your own life.

There are times in all our lives when we need help. It might be a charity or school that needs help, or someone we know, or even a perfect stranger. Charities are better at reaching out for help, as humans are sometimes reluctant to ask. When we see the need and step up to be of assistance, rarely are we turned away. When you donate to a registered charity, you will often get a tax deduction too, which ultimately helps you keep a little more money in your pocket, so you can give more in the future!

When we choose to help someone from the kindness of our heart—whether we saw a need or fulfilled someone's request for help—we feel good, and when we give without expectation of receiving something back, we feel even better. Giving to others feels good right down to the core of who you are.

A Giving Story by Lance

A cousin of mine who wishes to remain anonymous (so I'll call her Angela) uses the Mmm. Even though she has a limited income, she uses the Give Jar and donates the money whenever the right cause or reason strikes her fancy.

At the point in time this story occurred, Angela had saved up a tidy sum in her Give Jar and did not yet have a plan on how, who, or where she was going to share the funds.

One of our daughters was asked to represent Canada in a world dance competition in Germany. She and the other girls in her dance team had to do some fund-raising to help pay for a large portion of the travel costs AND find extra money for their personal expenses as well. There was a very short time line, and although our daughter worked very hard to create extra income, she knew she could not possibly save enough in time to fund the entire trip.

Before you question why we as her parents didn't step up to the plate and just pay for it, let me explain, we had our own costs to cover and there was very little time between the announcement of the opportunity and the trip departure date. We also saw this as a learning opportunity for our daughter. We told her if she wanted to go, she would need to ask for help to raise the money.

My extremely proud daughter announced to our entire extended family the team accomplishment of being asked to represent Canada and explained she needed help to reach her financial goals, so she could participate. She was not looking for handouts, but rather ideas on what she could do to earn some money.

Angela called us and said she wanted to give my daughter all the money she had in her Give Jar. My daughter was overwhelmed with the kindness shown to her. I asked Angela if she was sure she wanted to give this money to her. She responded with this statement: "Just as you said, Lance, being able to have money set aside to give when I wanted gave me such a great feeling. I knew I wanted to give it to someone in need, and that's what I had been saving it for. I just didn't know who it would be or why. I feel so lucky I can help her to represent Canada."

I can tell you this—the day our daughter and the dance team won at the World Competition was not just a win for Canada. It was a win for my daughter, my cousin, and me too!

The purpose of the Give Jar is to have money set aside to help others in need. There are many good causes and just as Angela helped our daughter in her time of need, each person will find the right time and place to use their Give Jar money.

You may choose to help a homeless person or an animal rescue center. Perhaps it will be a donation for research to cure a sickness or even help a family out of a tight spot they didn't foresee happening.

School-age kids are often asked to help raise money for programs at school or donate to help someone in their school. There are no right or wrong places to use the Give Jar money, or how much of it to use at one time. If it makes the person donating the money feel happy and fulfilled, it's the right thing to do.

Charity has many different forms and people and organizations need help in so many ways. When you manage your money with a system, and money is simply waiting for you to help when the right reason comes along, the feeling you will have is amazing. The money was there for this exact reason, so it will feel so good when you hand it over. Save to give—trust us, when you next hear the expression, "It is better to give than to receive," you will know exactly what we mean.

The YET Kids' Perspectives on the Give Jar

Kamryn, Age Ten

"When I first heard about the Give Jar, I was very excited. My first thought was that I could donate to places that help animals. I love animals. I use the money for other good causes, too. Once, I was at an event and someone there was raising money to help build a kitchen for an orphanage in Africa. I donated $100 and it made me smile to know I would be helping other kids. Right now, I'm saving up again to donate to the SPCA in our community."

Kai, Age Thirteen

"I thought it was exactly what it said—for giving or donating to others. I think it's the best jar of all, but I haven't used it yet, but I know that when the feeling is right, and I find the right place to donate, I'll have the money to give. I like that feeling."

Taya, Age Eleven

"Before learning about the Give Jar; I never ever thought about donating to good causes. When I learned about it, I thought it was a nice idea, but I thought you had to give all the money to one place at a time. Now I know I can donate how much I want, when I want, to whatever charity I want. Right now, I'm doing a school project about dogs that have been abused, so I have decided I want to save up even more money and donate it to a local animal shelter, so they can put the money into saving at least one dog from a bad home. I love animals, and I know that it's going to feel really good when I make that donation."

Shaqala, Age Fifteen

"I thought it was really kind, and I still feel the same. For me it's a good jar, and I like to make sure that I'm picking the right place and time to donate. I usually use my Give Jar money to the Children's Hospital. It makes me happy to *donate because I know I am helping out another person."*

Part 5

Chapter 23
Allowance Hour with Lance

I'm often asked exactly what happens at our house during Allowance Hour. Do we have rules, and do we change them or relax them in any way? Is it worth the headache of trying to coordinate everyone to be at the same place, at the same time?

The answer is absolutely 100 % YES to being worth the headache.

The time we spend with the kids talking about money has created some of our best learning opportunities and some fun times as well. As to exactly what happens? I thought it easiest to share the base of what happens in point form and address some of the other questions later in the book.

1. We gather our family around the kitchen table. Each kid is required to bring their money jars to the meeting.
2. We then ask each kid to work out how much they are owed for allowance. Each one is then given the correct amount, in cash, with a variety of small bills and coins. This is so they can practice handling a variety of bills and coins to allocate into each jar.
3. Each kid then must calculate how much of their allowance will get managed into the different jar categories in our Mmm system. This money is then distributed into their own set of money jars.
4. As a family, we also discuss if any additional money was earned or gifted in the previous two-week period and how they managed that money.

Earned Money

Earned money is not allowance money, but money earned from additional chores or working for someone outside the home. Earned money is also net profit from any of their entrepreneur or business ventures. All earned money must be divided into the Mmm system.

Gift Money

When the kids receive money as a gift, our rule is, they have the option of managing the gift money into the Mmm in the way it is designed—or, if they want to, they can divide or spend that gift money any way they want.

Handling Cash

We have learned having actual cash, which they handle and place into their jars, has created a better understanding of money and appreciation for money. We have also noticed our kids pay more attention when making purchases at stores to ensure they get the correct change.

For the balance of the hour, we talk about a topic related to money. Our discussion about money is very flexible; we use the opportunity to teach them about things like donations, interest, debt, taxes, how banking works, and credit cards. The more you talk openly about the topic of money with your kids, the more they will learn to handle it properly when they do start earning it. After all, you don't want them thinking money grows on trees!

TOP 10 Topics for Allowance Hour Discussion

1. Where does the family income come from? How often does the money get paid?
2. What are the fixed expenses in your home that must be paid every month i.e. mortgage or rent, taxes, house or tenant insurance, light, heat, water, healthcare insurance, daycare costs?
3. What are the variable expenses that must be paid every month i.e. basic phone bill, cable, internet, transportation, groceries?

4. What are the seasonal or occasional expenses that come up (clothing, shoes, birthdays, special events and holidays, school fees, sports or extracurricular program fees, dental visits, doctor's visits, eye glasses)?
5. What is the difference between a Want and a Need?
6. Who handles money responsibilities such as bill payments and shopping and why?
7. How do major money decisions get made in your home?
8. What are the various bank fees and types of bank accounts?
9. What is a debit card and how does it work?
10. What is a credit card and what are the benefits and pitfalls of using a credit card?

The YET Kids' Perspectives on Allowance Hour

Taya, Age Eleven

"At our house, my parents and I do talk about money quite a bit. They help me make sure I am using the jars properly, and they help me make decisions about if what I am about to purchase is a good idea. They also encourage me to read books, and we talk about what I'm reading. Right now, I'm reading Rich Dad, Poor Dad. It's a really good book. I read it at school during silent reading period. My friends are kind of confused by the books that I read, but they know I'm an entrepreneur, so it's OK."

Shaqala, Age Fifteen

"My parents and I talk about money stuff all the time. We discuss what my plans are and what I am planning to save for. We talk about other things too, like credit cards and bank fees. I'm not old enough to get a credit card yet, but when I am, I know that I would know enough not to spend over my limit and to pay it off every month."

Kamryn, Age Ten

"During our Allowance Hour, we talk about a lot of things. We talk about money that we earned or were given and how we will split that money into the different jars. We talk about how we managed our money, what we did right, or where we made mistakes to see what we can learn from them. We talk about things like taxes and bank fees. I'm excited because when I turn sixteen, I will be able to start using the Necessities of Life Jar, but I know that I'll still have the other jars like my Play Jar, Education Jar, and Plan to Spend Jar. My life is going to be pretty good then."

Kai, Age Thirteen

"We don't purposely sit down and talk about money every time. We do talk, though. My parents pay me to read books about money and write up a little report or notes. When I do that, we talk about what I have learned. The next book I am going to read is The Gumball Kid, *and*

after that I hope to read a book called Escape the Rat Race—*it's about how to become a Rich Kid by following Rich Dad's advice."*

Chapter 24

Do Your Kids Really Use Jars?

In Lance's home, the kids really use their own set of jars. They have decorated each jar with their name, the category, and the percentage of each category on the lid. They are all responsible to put the jars back in their designated space (they are not to be left lying around the house) after Allowance Hour and after taking out cash to make a purchase.

Tip: The jars do not all need to match (unless you are fashion-conscious or OCD).

Mason jars or pickle jars work just fine. If you have more than one kid and need to buy jars, the local dollar-type stores are a great source for finding decent-looking jars with well-fitting lids. Remember, the purpose here is to manage money, not spend a lot of it!

Teaching Kids to Handle Cash

Handling cash and making correct change is becoming a lost art. I recently made a purchase totalling $10.20. I handed the cashier a $20 bill and was in the process of looking for coins in my pocket when the cashier rang in $20 as the amount tendered. The till indicated $9.80 was the change that should be offered. I tried to give the cashier a quarter and politely requested, "Could you just give me back a $10 bill and a nickel? I have way too much change in my pocket right now."

The cashier almost had a mental meltdown—she had no idea what to do. She then called a supervisor over to help. The supervisor was also very confused and told me they were not allowed to accept the extra quarter and could only accept the $20 bill because it was too hard to make change. I kid you not—true story!

So, if you want your kids to be smarter than the average cashier, you will need to teach them this very basic skill.

Lance: My method is to pay attention to how many coins and bills they have in the jars. When I can see they have enough to make change with, I wait for them to tell me how much they require per the calculator and then I tell them I only have a larger bill than they need.

This forces them to give me back some change if they want their allowance. I ask them to figure out the bill I have, what they need, and what the difference is. Once they figure it out, they must find that amount in their jar and give it back to me in exchange for the bill I give them. This teaches them basic math skills and reinforces how to count money properly when giving or receiving change.

What If My Kids Want to Earn Extra Money?

Although we use the Allowance Money for Management method instead of the Allowance

Money for Chores method, we expect our kids to be regular contributing members of our household. They all have jobs to do on a daily or weekly basis, simply for the privilege of having a roof over their head and a belly full of food.

However, our kids love money! Once they have a goal for each jar, they are motivated to find ways to acquire more money, so they can reach their goal more quickly. They regularly ask if there are additional chores around the house that we might be willing to pay them to do.

There are almost always seasonal tasks or extra jobs we are happy to pay them for. For example, cleaning out the front hall closet, the broom closet, sorting out bathroom drawers and kitchen cupboards, washing windows, dusting blinds, raking leaves, or helping to prepare the yard in the spring. You get the picture.

We do allow them to take on additional chores when we need stuff done, but only after their regular chores are completed. However, the rule is that we consider this as earned money that must be distributed into their jars.

TOP Ten Chore Lists to Earn Extra Money at Home

1. Clean out the garage or storage shed
2. Wash or vacuum the family car
3. Clean and organize the kitchen or bathroom drawers
4. Sort and stack the linen closet
5. Wash windows or windowsills or spot wash walls
6. Help plant or weed the garden
7. Clean and organize the front or back hall closets
8. Clean and organize underneath the kitchen or bathroom sinks
9. Wash the dog or groom a pet
10. Help organize and file paperwork (such as bills and receipts) at home

Do You Allow Money to Be Moved from Jar to Jar?

The short answer to that question is NO! I'm often asked, "What if they had put their gift money into the Wealth Jar or Education Jar and later decide they want to spend it on a toy?"

The answer is still NO!

Gift money is the one source of money they can choose to do anything they want with. However, once they manage the money into their jar or jars of their choice, they can't change their mind and take it back out.

The rule of not moving money from jar to jar really makes them think long and hard about their choices and what they want. It's good practice for when they are older. What we have found is there are times when they may have just purchased something they had been saving up for using money from their Save to Spend Jar. They don't really have anything in mind they want anytime soon, so they make the choice to put the gift money into their Wealth or

Education Jar instead. Those are proud moments for us as parents.

How Do I Encourage My Kids to Put More Money into the Wealth Jar?

A colleague shared with me the following idea to reinforce the importance of the Wealth Jar to their kids and motivate them to manage more of their gift money into their personal Wealth Jar. We have since given this incentive to our own kids and it's working very well.

If you are in a financially stable place, you may want to encourage your kids to put money into their Wealth Jar by creating a, "Matching Money" or "Top Up" program.

When kids receive gift money they have the option of spending that money or managing it into any jar they like. When they choose to put some or all the money into their Wealth Jar, the parent can match that money on a percentage basis, dollar for dollar, or they can top up the amount to the nearest $5 or $10 or $20. In our house, we give an extra 50%, so if one of the kids takes $10 of gift money and puts into their Wealth Jar, we add an extra $5 as a reward for making a great financial decision.

This concept is like an employer matching what an employee puts into a forced retirement savings plan. I think it's a good way to encourage kids to see the importance you place on their future wealth.

Chapter 25
The Allure of Credit

When kids grow up without a steady source of money and then find themselves gifted with money (think birthday, Christmas, or even a lottery win), the sudden feeling of instant cash becomes a strong and powerful emotion. The allure of money is so strong we often indulge ourselves. We don't manage that money—we spend it! The same thing happens when they get their first paycheque—or two, or three, or four . . . you get the point.

Remember back to your first real paycheque? Chances are you lived at home or with roommates. You probably didn't have any debt to worry about, and yet what did you do? Likely you splurged on wants (clothes, dinners, cars, partying with friends) and did not manage that money for future needs, such as next week's groceries, your cell phone bill, or gas for your car. You felt rich, so you spent as though you were rich.

The challenge is once we get a taste of "the good life," it's hard to stop, and our society feeds that hunger. Advertising media is forever showing us things that supposedly will make our life better. We could simply be part of the "cool crowd" if we dress a certain way, drive a certain car, wear name brand goods, or take a winter vacation.

Banks and credit card companies also encourage us to live "the good life" and they make it so easy for us to do. Pre-approved credit card applications are mailed out stating, "Instant Credit"; social media has pop-ups such as, "Click here for Instant Approval on a Car Loan". We've even received advertising inserts in our credit card statements encouraging us to take on more credit, at an amazing low rate for the next ten months, including the ability to simply take money as a cash advance. Clearly society tends to tempt the Money Monster inside all of us—

easy to get credit, easy to get cash advances and so easy to spend tomorrow's money today.

"Are you Broke? Get Credit Here!" The marketing for credit never stops; after all, the more credit they give out, the more money banks and credit card companies can potentially make.

At most universities and colleges, credit card companies send teams of promoters to the campuses during the first few weeks of school. Often, they are young, trendy looking, and very friendly kids in the same age bracket. These promoters ask, "Would you like a credit card? Just fill out this application, and we will give you a free t-shirt for your favourite sports team!" Wow, there's a bonus. You get a potential lifetime of debt and a free t-shirt.

Not only are young people given the chance to blow the money they earned yesterday, but they are now encouraged to throw away the money they don't even have yet or will likely even earn in the next few years. Maybe instead of the free sports team shirt, the free t-shirt should read, "This person now owned by VISA" or "I now work for Mastercard FOREVER"!

Don't get us wrong—credit isn't a bad thing and in today's world, it can be worse to not have any credit than to have bad credit. However, we need to start teaching the next generation how to handle and manage credit or they will be destined to fail. We can begin by allowing our older kids to experience what borrowing with a credit card feels like by simulating that experience in the safety of their home, with parents who care about their future.

Chapter 26
Kids and Credit Cards

In this society, having no credit is almost worse than having bad credit. However, having access to credit and not knowing how to manage it can be devastating, with the results of fixing credit taking years to correct if not caught quickly!

The last thing we want to do is encourage our kids to get into a place where bad debt starts to ruin their life. So how do we teach them—and when? The answer is the sooner you can start to talk about how credit cards can be used wisely and how quickly they can turn into Money Monsters, the more likely it is that your children will be successful.

Almost anyone over the age of eighteen can qualify for a credit card. They usually start out with a small limit of $500 to $1,000. However, some credit card companies will increase the spending limit over time, without asking if the credit card holder even wants an increase.

We suggest you look at some of your older credit card statements; we bet you'll notice over time, they increased your limit without informing you or asking your permission.

Unfortunately, many kids see that "Magic Plastic" (a.k.a. credit card) as a step into adulthood and can't wait to get their first one. Without learning and using a money management system early in life, it doesn't take long for their bad debt to keep increasing. Before they know it, they owe more money than they could remember spending—which will be true, simply because the interest charged on unpaid balances piles up quickly.

Credit cards are one topic that must be discussed during Allowance Hour. It is critically important to know how interest is calculated and how much an item may really end up costing if you pay by credit card and don't pay it off within the interest-free period. It's also important to teach about extra fees that get applied. We have created the following fictional story to illustrate these points.

The Credit Card Lesson

This is the story of two friends Chris and Charlie, who have both moved away from home for the first time to go to college. They were both advised by their parents to be cautious with money, as they would only receive a monthly allowance to cover their basic needs while at school.

They are both approached on the first day of school by a pretty girl who signs them both up for a "no-fee credit card" with a "low interest rate" of 9%, and an interest-free period of thirty days. The credit card limit is $500.

Chris and Charlie are both excited to receive their new cards and they both go shopping and make purchases totalling $100. They love their new-found Magic Plastic credit cards—they feel so adultlike!

They both get their first credit card statement and Chris, who is a YET graduate pays his bill in full within the thirty-day interest-free period.

Charlie intended to pay his credit card bill in full within the thirty-day interest-free period; however, he had a little too much fun and overspent his monthly school allowance from home. He wants to be responsible and so he pays $99 of his bill, simply because that is all the money he had available.

Charlie feels good about his decision; he believes he owes only the $1.00 remaining and the 9% Interest on $1.00 is "not too much extra money"—it's only $.09, and he can easily pay off the $1.09 next month.

Before the next month credit card statement arrives, both Chris and Charlie need to buy more books for school totalling $500. They both use their Magic Plastic to make the purchase.

They both get their second credit card statement and once again Chris pays his bill within the thirty-day interest free period. He is building up a good credit record and being responsible with his money.

Sadly, Charlie did not understand how his credit card really worked. Since Charlie did not pay the entire balance from the month prior, the credit card company charged him interest on the entire $100 he had charged, and his new statement tells him that he now owes a dollar as a balance forward from the previous month plus $500 from buying books in month two. In addition, a $30 service charge has been added, and the interest payable is in the amount of $9 for a total of $540.

Charlie is confused and concerned. Once again, he does not have enough money to pay the credit card bill off in full. He pays $525 and decides he will not use his credit card this month. Charlie is now realizing the "Magic Plastic" he was so happy to receive might be, "Black Magic Plastic," as he is going into the red financially. Charlie is smart enough to know something is wrong and he asks Chris to help him understand.

Chris explains to Charlie, "If you do not pay off the ENTIRE amount of your purchases each month, the credit card company will charge you interest on the ENTIRE amount that was due and payable." Charlie was being charged interest of $9 on the $100 purchases he made in the first month, not just $.09 on the $1.00 he had not yet paid.

Chris goes on to explain because Charlie went OVER his maximum credit limit of $500, the credit card company did him a favor! The credit card company was being very kind to Charlie. When Charlie went to pay for his books, his credit card would have been rejected as his limit was $500 and he had a balance forward from the previous month.

The credit card company did not want Charlie to be embarrassed in front of the cashier—so as a "courtesy" to Charlie, they allowed him to buy the books, knowing this purchase would put him over the maximum limit they had told him he could charge. However, the "courtesy" came at a price of a $30 service fee.

Charlie was both mad and frustrated, as well as a little embarrassed he wasn't as smart as Chris. Charlie's parents had never taught him how to manage money or talked to him about credit card use and he was learning quickly that credit was not all fun and games.

Charlie phoned the credit card company and asked them to please not permit any future charges that would put him over the spending limit of $500 for which he was approved. He also asked them to remove the $30 service fee. They replied they could not remove the fee nor would they monitor his limit for him—that was his responsibility.

Chris suggested Charlie not make any more credit card purchases until he could truly understand how credit cards and all their charges worked. Charlie reluctantly agreed and set aside the $15 he would need to pay off the next statement.

Charlie received his third credit card statement and quickly realized he was a slow learner. He had forgotten the credit card *company was going to charge him on the entire amount owed from the month before. His interest payment was now $54, and he still had the balance from the month prior of $15. Charlie now owed them $69.*

Charlie expressed his rising frustration and asked Chris to help him really understand and learn about credit cards. Charlie was now committed to becoming as smart as Chris about credit use.

Moral of the Story: Don't Be a Charlie

Teach your kids about credit cards through stories or examples they can relate to. Use paper and pencil so they can erase errors as they are learning and have them calculate the numbers you talk about. Feel free to use Chris and Charlie as a starting point, although for younger kids you may need to proceed slowly and step-by-step to ensure they understand each element of the story.

Chapter 27

Should You Allow Your Kid to Have a Debit or Credit Card?

As we stated earlier in the book, if you want to learn about hockey, you need to get on the ice. If you want to learn to manage money, you need cash in hand to manage. So, it only makes logical sense if you want to teach kids about debit or credit cards, you need to make debit and credit cards available.

However, we all know kids are not financially educated enough to handle a real set of cards. As a result, we suggest you set up an opportunity for them to simulate the real-life experience or it is not going to be very beneficial to them.

On both of our websites www.YETTraining.com and www.MoneyMonsterOrMoneyMaster.com, you can purchase a kid-friendly set of "Magic Plastic Debit Card and Credit Cards" to help teach your kids the responsible use of each of these forms of payment.

Alternatively, you can make your own cards at home from a heavy paper or card stock. Just make sure the cards you make are sturdy enough for kids to use and will not rip or tear easily. The point is to establish the rules for each card and how it is to be used.

The following chapters will go into more detail about how to help your kids learn about how debit card use, credit card use, and loan agreements work.

Chapter 28
Debit Card Rules

As with all things in life, rules make the world go around and are simply a necessity for a civilized society. Rules around debit card and credit card use in the Mmm system and in your home will have the same outcome: an easier place to live and have open discussions without chaos.

Prior to allowing your child the privilege of using a debit card, rules must be established, a process created, and both fully understood prior to receiving the card. Make this a great learning opportunity by writing these rules down together and then getting your kids to sign an agreement that states they understand ad agree to what has been discussed.

Debit Card Rules

1. They must be in possession of the debit card to use it.

2. If they cannot remember their personal Secret Pin Code* — It cannot be used.
3. If the card is lost or stolen, a $5 per card reissue fee must be paid before a new card is provided.
4. Cash payment from the correct jar must be made as soon as they get home, or the parent gets to keep the goods.

***Secret Pin Code**: We suggest for each debit card you issue to your kids, you also give them a Secret Pin Code they must remember and provide to you prior to using the card. This process would be the same experience as in the real world: no pin, no purchase.

Hint: Use the reverse of their month and year of birth so you can easily remember which kid owns which Secret Pin Code, but do not tell them how you came up with the Pin Code.

> **DEBIT Card:**
>
> DEBIT CARD issued to: _Your Child's
>
> **Name**_____
>
> **Payment Terms**: Cash Payment MUST be made from the correct Jar upon return home.

Debit Card Use

Incorporate the use of their debit card with the Mmm Jar System in your home. If, while out shopping with you, one of the kids wants to make a purchase and they can show you their debit card and give you the correct Secret Pin Code, you can purchase the item for them.

When you get home, they must then take the money from the correct jar and pay the amount in full on the receipt and then you can release possession of the item purchased to them.

As your kids get older and more experienced with their debit card, you may want to introduce the concept of having their own credit card.

Chapter 29
Credit Card Rules

Since credit card use can really start the early onset of Money Monster behavior, it is doubly important to establish a clear understanding between you and your child prior to giving them a credit card to learn with. We do not advocate the use of the credit card process until they have successfully used and understood the debit card system for a reasonable period and until they are mature enough to completely understand how the numbers will be calculated and the impact poor money management can potentially have on their finances.

Once again, this is a learning opportunity meant to set them up for success, which means a written agreement must be created and signed by all parties prior to receiving the card.

Credit Card Rules

1. They must be in possession of the credit card to use it.
2. If they cannot remember their personal Secret Pin Code*—it cannot be used.
3. If the card is lost or stolen, a $5 per card reissue fee must be paid before a new card is provided.
4. Credit card purchases may only be used for items in the following categories: Necessities of Life, Education, Save to Spend, or Play Jars. They may not be used to make donations or for Wealth Jar purchases.

Before introducing any card use to your kids, you must first establish the terms for borrowing money. Write down the terms on the card itself as a visual reminder of your discussion.

Ensure they fully understand what each term means and the consequence it will create on their future income. After all, you are now teaching them what spending tomorrow's allowance will feel like when it's time to pay back the money in the future.

1. Monthly Interest Rate – We suggest a minimum of 10% per month. Note: we realize banks charge an annual interest fee; however, the point of this teaching is to allow kids to see how quickly interest charges add up.
2. Payment Terms: Thirty days interest-free from the day of purchase
3. Limit: Based on your own good judgement
4. Over Limit Fee: We suggest $10

Magic Plastic CREDIT Card:

Issued to: **Your Child's Name**_____

Monthly Interest Rate: _____

Payment Terms: _____

Credit Limit: _____

Over Limit Fee: _____

As with the debit card program, if your kid wants to make a purchase and they can show you their credit card and provide the correct Secret Pin Code, you can purchase the item for them.

When you get home, the receipt is placed into the appropriate jar the item would have been purchased from if they had available cash. The word CREDIT CARD must be written on the back of the receipt.

During the next Allowance Hour, they must calculate how much of their allowance would normally go into that jar, and that amount of allowance is deducted from the back of the receipt. If the receipt is small in size, you may want to attach a piece of note paper to the receipt.

If they are not able to pay for the receipt in full within thirty days, at the next Allowance Hour, they will then need to calculate the interest payable on the full amount of the receipt and backdated to the date of purchase—just like a credit card company would do in the real world.

Interest payable is then added to the total on the back of the receipt, and a new payable amount is established.

Repeat the process each Allowance Hour, either increasing the interest payable or reducing the amount owed, depending upon how much is paid. When the amount is paid in full, the receipt can come out of the jar.

If your child has had to pay interest, we strongly suggest together you add up the amount of money paid in interest plus the original purchase price, and then discuss if the use of the credit card was a wise decision. Was the item a Need or a Want? If it was purchased on sale, did the final cost including interest charges exceed the regular price? This conversation is not intended to belittle your child, but rather is meant to be a learning opportunity and create conversations to help them to best manage future money decisions.

This is a simple way to show them what spending tomorrow's money today feels like. It's easy to buy on credit . . . not so much fun paying it back.

Credit and Wealth Jar Purchases

Lance: I like to encourage our kids to be entrepreneurial and grow their Wealth Jar. If they come to me with a solid idea of what they can do to grow their Wealth Jar, but they need a bit of extra money to make a purchase for supplies or other costs, I will provide them with an interest-free loan. We take the time to write out an interest-free loan agreement, stating the amount borrowed, what it is to be used to purchase, and the commitment that they will pay me from the profits of their business venture and from future allowances until the loan is paid in full. That agreement is then placed in their Wealth Jar.

Chapter 30
Loaning Money to Kids

There may come a time when it will make sense to you and your child to negotiate a real loan. This is likely when they are in their late teens or early adult years and require funds for a larger purpose, such as a school travel event, their first car, or perhaps even additional education such as trade school, college, or university.

Have an open discussion to clearly establish what you are loaning the money for, why you have chosen to give them the privilege of a loan, and what the consequences will be in the future if they make late payments or miss making payments to you.

This would be a really great time to introduce to them how credit scores work in the real world. Explain how a simple late payment can create a future higher interest rate on their next purchase—or worse yet, how continued late or missed payments will affect their ability to borrow from many sources. If you are not familiar with how credit scores are calculated, this is an excellent time for you to do some research on your own. Many banks have online credit score information or you can simply Google "how do credit scores work" and you will find plenty of information.

Once you have decided on the amount of the loan and the terms you are willing to provide, write up the loan agreement, including the interest rate, when and how often payments are to be made, and what the consequences will be for late or missed loan payments. Make sure you both sign and keep a copy of the paperwork.

Lance: Since I would only make a loan to my kids if I believed in its purpose, I give them a period of time when the loan is made to them interest-free.

If the loan is not paid back in full, or a late payment or missed payment occurs, then the interest-free agreement is void and I start charging them the pre-arranged interest rate (a low but manageable rate compared to a bank). If they again fail to make a payment on time or miss a payment, the interest rate is increased substantially.

My purpose is not to make money from my kids, but to help them understand there are consequences for their actions, or lack of action. If I see they are spending money on things that are, in my opinion, wasteful or doing things that are not a good use of their time as it relates to creating an income to pay me back, I remind them I might not be so willing to help them again in the future. I don't mind helping my kids, but I won't be taken advantage of either.

Part 6

Chapter 31

Mmm Sounds Good—How Can I Make This Work in My Money Monster-Filled Life?

We're hoping by this point in the book you, as an adult, will also convert your money management style to living with the Mmm system. The challenge for most people is they cannot easily live within the percentages we suggest. The hardest category to imagine living within is usually the Necessities of Life Jar at 55% of your net income.

However, we don't think you are like most people. After all, you purchased this book to help your kids, and you've read through it to this chapter. We presume you are now smart enough to ask, "What if I can't live within the 55% of my net income? Where do I get the rest of the money to live on—or what jar do I omit?"

These are great questions and smart ones to ask. We wish we had an easy answer for you and could simply wave a magic wand to turn your life around. Unfortunately, we don't.

We really want to say, "It's not your fault," as we know in most cases you were never taught a system of how to manage money. However, that isn't going to be of help to you now. The reality is this: If you want things to change in your life, you must change things in your life.

Why Should You Want to Make a Change?

There are a couple of great reasons you should want to make a change in your financial life. The greatest reason is your family relationships. Did you know most marriages break up because of money problems? Learning to use the Mmm may save your relationship if you are married, and if you are not yet married, at the very least becoming financially free will make your current or future relationship a lot more fun.

You will also want to set an example for your kids to follow. After all, if you had been taught a money management system when you were younger, you would not be in the position you are today. You would have learned to think twice before making the many financial choices that put you where you are at this moment. Your kids will follow your example.

The third reason to want to make a change is for your own emotional health. Feeding the Money Monster, the feeling of dread when you get mail, or even answer your phone in case it is a debt collector are all things that can be turned around if you start to make the changes we suggest.

Likely the choices you made in the past were easy to make. You wanted that nice new car—a car loan was easy to get, and you bought it. The big screen TV? Yeah, likely came on credit too. Your latest cell phones? No problem—the companies that provide cell service made it easy to buy, and you could pay for them over time with their cell phone contract.

As you are already experiencing, it was super easy to get into debt, but the solution to get out is not so easy. You should be motivated to make a change today to live a better life—not just for tomorrow, but forever!

We know from our past that living with bad debt on a daily basis can suck the joy of life right out of you. However, gaining control of your financial life is a great feeling and one we want you to have, as well.

The good news is, it's not hard to start the process and once started, you will quickly move into a better financial position and emotional state than you are right now. You will start to feel better knowing you are on your way to having an easier time than you've had in the past.

Chapter 32

What is the First Step for Moving Forward?

There are only two ways to learn to live within the Necessities of Life Jar at 55% of your net income—neither one will come easily, but both are worthwhile to consider. Simply put, you can either make more money or spend less money.

We do not suggest the first thing you need to do is work harder, get a second job, or work overtime. Quality of life is important too and there are only so many hours in a week any person can put into creating money.

The first step is to figure out where you are spending your existing money. After all, if you don't know what is really happening with your money, you cannot begin to make good decisions. You cannot fix what you cannot identify.

Likely the reality of where you are financially may scare the pants off you. Like most people, you may choose to give up and live a life in financial hell until bankruptcy takes over, your spouse leaves you, or you get so stressed out you finally are motivated to make a change.

We hope that is not the case. You deserve a better life. Living with debt and stress is expensive both for your relationships and for your health.

Create a Spending Summary

On our website, you can download a FREE pdf or Excel spreadsheet called a Spending Summary. You can use it to start tracking your debt, your spending, and your income. If you are part of a committed relationship, both you and your partner will need to keep track of the money coming in and out of each of your wallets and personal bank accounts.

At the end of each week or at least once a month, combine your two summaries to get a true and accurate picture of how much you are spending and in what areas of your life.

This may sound like a pain in the butt (and truthfully it can be annoying at first); however, the effort is well worth the outcome. To make it easier, you may want to consider downloading a free app on your phone to help with the process of tracking the day-to-day receipts such as coffee, meals out, fuel purchases for your car, etc. Check out the App called "Mvelopes" or "Goodbudget" both of which are free and can be used on either Android or IOS.

Once you have done your first Spending Summary, it will get easier each time. Many of the numbers required will be consistent each month, and you will simply be updating your daily and weekly expenditures.

Norma: I now love our Spending Summary worksheet and use it every month. It is a great indication of our true costs of living and helps me to plan for our future. Several behavioural economists believe the mere act of monitoring expenses tends to reduce spending—even with people who were not planning to spend less. It tends to make them more financially aware on a subconscious level. I have found this statement to be true in my own life.

If you prefer, you can also visit either one of our websites for a FREE Downloadable version that is already set up and ready for you to use as an Excel spreadsheet. Visit us at www.MoneyMonsterorMoneyMaster.com or www.YETTraining.com

The hardest part of moving forward is looking at the current reality. You will need to look at all outstanding credit, all bank accounts, and all income. Before you decide you need to get another job, the next step will be to look at your current expenses and probably make some cuts, perhaps even some drastic cuts - some of which might be more painful than others.

Chapter 33
Lower Your Expenses

Now that your Spending Summary has been completed, the next step is to see where you can lower some of your expenses. To lower expenses, remember small things add up. Look at your day-to-day expenses. There are many things you can do to reduce a little here and there, but you will be surprised at how quickly they add up over a year.

You may have heard of the, "Latte Factor," a phrase coined by David Bach, a well-known American financial writer. The "Latte Factor" refers to how spending money on seemingly small amounts add up to large numbers over time. For example, what would happen if every day you stopped at a Starbucks or coffee shop and bought a fancy coffee? Let's presume the cost of that fancy coffee or latte is just $4. If you stop at a coffee shop every work day, five days a week, that coffee adds up to over $1000 per year. Imagine if you and your life partner both had the same habit—$2,000 a year literally has been swallowed up from your hard-earned money.

Do you take a lunch to work every day? Most people splurge at least three times a week on a store-bought or restaurant lunch. At a cost of $15 per lunch, that's over $2,250 a year. Multiply that by two people in your household and a cost of $4,500 is realized.

Dinner out two to three times a week? An average dinner can run $50 per couple with tax and tip included. Multiply that by fifty-two weeks a year and $7,800 just slips out of your fingers. Becoming aware of these "Latte Factors" is a necessary step in making choices on how to best manage your money. Small changes in behavior or habits can add up to big savings over time. For example, consider eating at home more often or changing what you order when dining out. We have friends who decided to stop ordering beverages when they dined out;

instead they enjoy a glass of water with lemon. With their family of six, it automatically reduced their meal costs by $18 to $24 every time they went to a restaurant!

We do not want you to stop enjoying some of life's little pleasures, but you may want to seriously look at the money you are spending on food and beverage outside your home.

The three items above equate to spending over $14,000 a year. Just by cutting back half of those, "Latte Factor"-type expenses, you could have an extra $7,000 to pay down debt.

Entertainment and electronics are two other areas you could potentially save some costs. You say you never go out, but stay at home and watch TV? Consider cutting back or even cancelling your cable or satellite TV. Who truly needs 300 channels anyway? You can choose to live with a basic cable package or you could start using Netflix or another similar service. Place the savings into debt repayment. You might also consider starting up a regular

Friday or Saturday night to play board games or card games with family and friends. Saving money and building up your relationships is a great way to enhance your life.

If you have not recently reviewed your cell phone plans, now would be a good time to do so. Do you really need a landline as well? What about that fitness or gym membership? Is it necessary or could you work out at home?

If you are really feeling the financial pinch and you own a home, consider the option of downsizing. A bigger house does not make a happier home. Just make sure you look at all the numbers before you sell your house. Are there penalty payouts for your mortgage you need to consider? If you live in an apartment, can you move to a less expensive place?

Consider your transportation costs as an area to reduce expenses. When was the last time you reviewed your insurance policy? Do you still need full coverage on a car that is five- or ten-years-old?

If you are driving a car with high car payments, consider trading in your fancy luxury car for a more standard one. We don't mean something that will break down, because that will just cost you more in the end, but something reliable without so many bells and whistles. If you have more than one car in your household, perhaps selling one of them and using the money to pay down some debt is a possibility. You'll not only pay down bad debt, but you'll also reduce your monthly out-of-pocket costs. Taking public transportation, using a taxi, or renting a car is often cheaper than owning a second vehicle.

Chapter 34
Increase Cash Flow

The flip side of reducing expenses is increasing the money you bring in. We know working more hours is likely the last thing you want to do. But is what you are doing now truly working in your life?

A short-term period of working a bit extra now can drastically shorten how long it will take you to remove the Money Monster from your life. This will automatically increase the cash you have available to live and allow you to start using the entire Mmm system—including building a wealth account for tomorrow.

Consider what else you can do to create a bit more cash. As silly and as obvious as this may sound, there are always people looking for casual help if you look around. A great spot to find them is on local social media sites such as

Facebook. People are often needing someone to help take loads of garbage to the dump, shovel their walks in the winter, or mow their yard in the summer. Some need help with moving, painting their house, staining a fence, or even watching their kids before or after school. Pet care, walking dogs, or even pet sitting, or house sitting are also possibilities.

 Many older people are looking for a little bit of extra help with things such as putting up shelves, making meals to put in the freezer, or seasonal tasks like gardening. These are all tasks that can serve another human being in their time of need, make you feel better, and put a little extra cash in your bank account.

 You can offer your services by posting notices on local billboards, making and delivering a few inexpensive flyers to your community neighbours, or posting your availability on local social media sites. Get creative—after all, your financial freedom is at stake!

An additional source of income you may want to consider is a home-based business or network marketing company. There are many to choose from. Just ensure the one you choose has products or services you can believe in. Even though I was already financially free (meaning more passive income than expenses), I continued to help others find financial freedom through a couple of companies I believe in. Don't be afraid to explore a multiple of options and ideas. There is everything from healthcare products, makeup, jewelry, and even e-currency education available as a second source of income.

Lastly, look around your home, your yard, and your garage. Do you also have a storage locker full of stuff? Check inside it as well. What about selling some of the recreational toys you own? If you are financially upside down, doesn't it make sense to consider your surfboard, golf clubs, bikes, and skis as things you could sell now to help pay down some of that debt?

Take a good look through your clothes closets and every nook and cranny around your home. With the use of social media, selling clothes, toys, and other items is relatively easy. You get to declutter your life at the same time as you pay down debt with the proceeds of the sales.

We know it's not easy parting with something you love or paid "good money" for. But you are paying more and more for those same items every day because of the cost of interest on the unpaid debts you owe. You can always buy back the items later that you really want and need—but you'll enjoy them more knowing you paid cash for them.

Consider making a change to your living arrangements. A bigger home does not mean a better or happier life. If you can't sell or downsize your home, use your home to create some extra income. Check out social media sites like www.AirBnB.com to see how they work; look at housing an international student from a nearby school or university. Bring in a housemate or roommate. These ideas can make a big difference in reducing your monthly housing costs.

Perhaps you have extra space in your yard or driveway and can rent space to store someone's boat or trailer. Look at all the options around you.

Whatever extra income you can bring in, use it to pay down bad debt, which will ultimately increase your monthly cash flow. You will quickly find your way back on the happy track of good finances.

The Reality of Making Changes

You may need to both reduce expenses and increase your income at the same time. Just remember, the first step to getting out of a debt hole is to stop digging the hole. The next step is to find a way to climb out. We hope you will consider these suggested changes as small but effective ladders. They are only short-term sacrifices, but in the end, you and your family will be much happier and enjoy life once you are back in balance and out of the debt hole forever.

Chapter 35
Insanity

The definition of insanity is doing the same thing repeatedly and expecting a different result. If we don't step back and look at things differently, we cannot see or stop the insanity cycle.

Lance: I'm someone who likes to look back at things and rethink them. In my mind, life sometimes feels like we are riding on a passenger train chugging along the tracks. We get lulled by the easy motion of the train, we watch life go by, we enjoy the scenery, and we enjoy the ride. We are moving forward without a lot of thinking and very little reflection.

The real lessons are learned when you get off the train and look back at it while it's moving by. You realize there's more to life than what you see sitting in the window seat looking out. I look for those moments.

When I was young I wanted to be rich. I

wanted to have anything and everything. Money would be no object. If I could dream it, I would have it. I didn't know how it would happen, but I did know since I had chosen to be rich, then I would be rich. I believed being rich would just happen.

Guess what? I was wrong.

I fell for the same trap as most young adults do. I got the good job, I made the money, and I spent, spent, spent. I was feeding the Money Monster and the Monster was always hungry. Eventually I realized I wasn't getting rich this way. I had to get off the train and look back. I then realized simply believing I would be rich was not enough to make it happen. If I continued to do the same things I was doing, I would never become wealthy. I'd like to share the following story with you to help you really understand what I am talking about.

Floyd the Fly

Imagine a fly at a window. We'll call him Floyd. Floyd keeps buzzing and buzzing against the glass, hoping eventually he will somehow get through that window. When Floyd gets tired, he stops for a moment and looks down. He can see all the other flies have died—the ones that never made it through the window—laying there at the bottom on the windowsill.

Floyd decides he won't be like them. He can see the other flies on the outside, buzzing about and enjoying life. Floyd wants to be like those flies. Those flies are lucky, he thinks. He becomes even more determined to find a way through the window. He becomes more persistent; he works harder at getting through the glass. Unfortunately for Floyd he fails and eventually he dies from working so hard.

Floyd died because he continued to do the same thing over and over . . . never finding freedom. Floyd's actions and results were the true definition of insanity.

Had Floyd simply flown back a few feet and stopped to review what was happening, or if Floyd had sought out a mentor fly to show him what to do, he could have looked back, and things would have been much different.

Floyd would have been able to make a simple observation—you see, just a few feet to the right of the glass window was an open door.

He could have discovered a path to freedom; he could have found his way to a better life. He could have spent his life buzzing around in the sunshine and fresh air—and not resigned himself to a painful death of repeating the same pattern over and over and over again.

Moral of the Story: Don't Be a Floyd!

Life doesn't have to be hard.

We just need to learn a different way. Sometimes it means getting off the train and looking back—figuring out what is working in your life and, more importantly, what is not. Once you can see the track you are on is not getting you where you want to be, you can ask for help. You can find books, videos, and mentors to help you find a better path.

In our personal experience, we've found successful people have almost always been willing to help us learn and to teach us if we were prepared to act on any advice they offered.

If your mind is open enough to acknowledge you might need a little guidance; if you are willing to become a little "uncomfortable" and try new things; if you strive to accept new ideas and really give these ideas a try—you too can find an open door, where perhaps a glass window had been holding you back.

Lance: I love learning new things. I wasn't a great student at school. I struggled my way through. Perhaps what they were teaching was just not stuff I wanted to learn, or perhaps my mind wasn't prepared to be uncomfortable, or perhaps I wasn't willing to ask for help when I needed it.

At one point, I realized I needed to stop the pattern of what I was doing, or I would never be rich. I decided to get off the train. I looked back and I decided to learn more. I purposely searched out people who had more than me, who started where I was, who I could ask for guidance and help. I suggest everyone step off the train and do the same in their life.

Chapter 36

Financially Overwhelmed? Know You Need to Take Action?

After reviewing all your expenses and income, reducing some costs and adding a bit more cash to your life, you still think you can't live on 55% of your monthly take home pay—don't panic or give up! Seriously, we know how hard it is to make a major change and clearly you must continue to pay your true necessities of life, including the bad debt you accrued in the past.

We still want you to continue to review and reduce your expenses and increase your income as time goes on. However, what is most important at this moment is that you take a small step forward toward your goal of creating change toward an easier life and using the Mmm System in your own home.

We have a relatively easy solution, so you can at least start moving away from the debt hole you are in and start to move the Money Monster out of your life. Starting to act toward your goals of establishing new and good money habits will automatically help you to start thinking and feeling differently about your finances.

Learning to think more positively about your money situation is an important part of this process. Action combined with good thoughts brings good results.

The first steps to changing your current reality is to change your attitude and that begins with gratitude. If becoming grateful for what you now have in your life is not already part of your daily routine, this is where we would like to you start. And it's simple to do!

Each morning before you start your busy day, take two or three minutes and think about the things in your life you are grateful for. These might be little things, like having hot water to enjoy a morning shower with, having food in the fridge to feed your family, or enough money to buy gas to get to work for the day.

Next think about your personal life and what and who you are grateful for there, as well. You might think of family members, coworkers, and friends. You may think about the love you have in your home, or your healthy children. You may feel grateful you have a job, for there are many people who only wish they could be employed.

Whatever you choose to feel grateful for in the moment is the perfect thought for you. Positive thoughts bring more positive results into your life.

When times are tough financially, it's easy to dwell in the land of negativity. Thinking positive thoughts of gratitude every day will help you move forward to a better life and a healthier mindset, as well.

Enough of the Warm Fuzzy Stuff—Time to Move Forward with a Plan of Attack

We want you to start using the Mmm System in a modified way. There is never a perfect time to move forward with any changes, however moving forward toward change is important. We want you to establish a set amount of money you can work with on each payday to use in the Mmm system as the starting point of moving toward financial freedom.

For purpose of this discussion, we'll use $100 as the amount. We want you to set up a group of clear glass jars and mark them with each category, including the Necessities of Life Jar. Each time you get paid, take $100 in cash and manage the money according to the percentages we suggest, placing the cash in each category.

It's the physical action that will help you move toward your goal more so than the dollar amount you choose. If you can only afford $20, then use that amount. The reason we say this is that money attracts money, and you need to start establishing good money management behaviors.

Every few months, take the Necessities of Life Jar and use that money to pay down your bad debt. We want you to use the other jars as they are intended. Once you begin treating your money in this manner, more of the good energy around managing your money will show up in your life.

We both attended the same business conference where we heard the following story about a single mom we'll call Betty. Her story is a perfect illustration of what we are sharing with you.

The Bubble Gum Story

Betty was a single mom who learned about a money management system. She was desperately broke, struggling day by day, but she knew she needed to make a change in her financial mindset. She decided to participate by setting aside $1.00 a month. Yep, one single dollar.

She was determined to find her way to financial freedom and followed a jar system, using her single dollar. In the system she learned, the rule was she had to spend the Play Jar money every thirty days.

This meant she would have only $.10 to spend. She thought long and hard about what she could do that would be fun, and she finally decided on buying two pieces of Double Bubble Bubble Gum, one for her and one for her son.

Remember those small pieces of bright pink bubble gum wrapped up as a square shape? Remember how they had a cartoon inside, as well?

Betty and her son, Bobby, who was then just seven-years-old, needed some fun and laughter in their life. Betty made an event out of going to the store and searching out two perfect pieces of gum from the plastic display bowl.

They then went to the park and found a shady spot to sit and rest. Together they slowly *unwrapped each piece of Double Bubble Bubble Gum. They read the comic wrapper out loud to each other and had a little giggle or two. They then had a bubble blowing contest between the two of them.*

Later in life, Bobby told her that was one of his favorite memories as a young kid. He told her how he knew they had no money, but she created a time for them to be together and simply be goofy and have a good time.

As volunteers at these types of events, we have met many people just like Betty. Although we have no idea how this Betty is doing financially now, we can tell you the other people we have met are living much happier lives—simply because they were committed to learning a better way to manage money and create money attraction habits.

Moral of the story: Be like Betty.

Change your life, one dollar at a time.

Chapter 37

Pay Yourself First to Reach Financial Freedom

The world around us is changing. Most of us were taught both in school and by our parents to do well in school and get a good, steady job with good pay. Pay off our mortgage. Save for retirement. Invest in a retirement savings plan. They believed we could then retire at sixty-five and live out our lives without worries or concern.

Those statements were all true at one point in time. Unfortunately, our world has changed and is changing faster every day. What we were taught in the past is just not true anymore.

If you look carefully at today's workforce, you will likely notice much older employees in what used to be considered entry-level positions. Many of these people are working because they must, not because they want to.

Unless you want to be working well into your senior years, that is the reality you will be facing if you don't stop the Money Monster. The way to stop the Money Monster is to change your current spending patterns.

Earlier in this book we talked about mentors and how a book can be the start of mentorship for some people. There are three books we have read and recommend to others. All three books and authors have one common concept. The concept is simple: Pay yourself first. Each author may use words in a different way, however the intention is the same. Let us share with you what we've understood and how we apply the concept.

The first book was written by David Chilton and is called *The Wealthy Barber*. He has recently released an updated version called *The Wealthy Barber Returns*, also highly recommended, as it is twenty years' worth of his wisdom in an easy-to-understand and entertaining read.

The one lesson we both understood when we read David Chilton's first book was that it's important to pay yourself first. This means putting money away for savings and investing and spend the rest living life wisely. Unfortunately, we were both slow learners. We paid our bills first, lived life second and never had enough money left at the end of the month to save.

In his most recent edition, Chilton writes, "Save first. Spend the rest. Good. Spend first, Save the rest. Bad. It really is that straightforward." Simple words, but simple works! It is now one of our most guided principles and the reason for using a Wealth Jar.

The second book of great influence was written by T. Harv Eker, *Secrets of the Millionaire Mind*. This book helped us to identify the thoughts we had about money that were no longer beneficial to keep. It's a great read on the mindset of money and how to change your past money memories. It has been truly a life changer for both of us.

In his book, T. Harv Eker writes, "Open a separate bank account designated your Financial Freedom Account. Put 10 percent of every dollar you receive (after taxes) into this fund. This money is only to be used for investments and buying or creating passive-income streams."

The other book? Likely not a surprise to you at this point; it's *Rich Dad, Poor Dad,* by Robert Kiyosaki. Like David Chilton, Robert Kiyosaki has also released a new version that includes updates for today's world and nine new study session sections. We have bought multiple copies of both the original version and the updated one and given them to people that we care about over the years. Truly life changing!

Robert Kiyosaki also strongly advocates paying yourself first in both editions, and he gives credit for that phrase to George Clason's book, *The Richest Man in Babylon*, of which millions of copies have been sold.

In his most recent edition, Kiyosaki writes, "Now, I can hear the howls from those of you who sincerely believe in paying your bills first. And I can hear all the responsible people who pay their bills on time. I am not saying be irresponsible and not pay your bills. All I am saying is do what the books says, which is: Pay yourself first."

He goes on to explain if occasionally you come up short with money to pay your bills, you still need to pay yourself first. We are paraphrasing here, but our words convey his intention.

If collectors start to call you for unpaid bills, they are doing you a favor; they are pushing you around. You will be motivated to find the money to pay your bills. Your investing and savings account will never yell at you for not paying yourself first, and yet it is imperative to have money to invest, so eventually you never have to deal with a creditor again.

We also love and appreciate all the Rich Dad and Rich Dad Advisors' books, as they were the first books that really helped us start our journey to financial education and where we first began to really understand cash flow and passive income.

We hope by sharing with you our favorite three mentors and their common viewpoint we are motivating you to start using the Mmm, including the Wealth Jar to pay yourself first. We are so very passionate on this subject because it is your Wealth Jar money that you will eventually use to help you create passive income.

Chapter 38
Passive Income

What exactly is Passive Income? Many people have their own definition, but we thought we would check out Google, and here is what we found:

> *"Investopedia defines* **Passive Income** *as,* "earnings an individual derives from a rental property, limited partnership or other enterprise in which he or she is not actively involved." *Popular culture, however, defines it as,* "any money you earn while sitting on a beach, sipping mojitos."

We both loved the part about sitting on a beach and sipping on a mojito; and we admit, we both live our lives in such a way that we get more beach time than the general population. We love owning passive income investments.

Simply put, passive income is money you earn without exchanging your time or labor to earn. We know that may sound odd for some of you, so we've created a couple of simplistic examples for you below:

A friend of yours purchases a nice little fishing boat. He lives in a condo. He didn't thoroughly think the purchase through and at the end of the fishing season, he realizes the condo board does not permit recreational vehicles to be parked on-site. He approaches you and asks if he can park his boat at your home. He offers to pay you $100 a month. The $100 per month would be considered passive income, as you don't need to trade your time or labour to earn that money.

Remember the story about Lucas, The Gumball Kid? His business was an example of passive income as well. He owned a gumball machine he placed in a retail business. Day after day, people put quarters in the machine. He would go to the retail business once a month and refill the gumballs and collect the money from the machine. If he spent $30 on the cost of his gumballs and collected $100 in cash, his passive income would be $70 from each machine.

Passive income is where you do not have to regularly trade your time or labour to earn money. It is where your money works for you, instead of you working for the money. In Lucas' example, he placed his money into buying a machine and stocked it with candy.

Now, we can already hear some of you thinking, *Yeah, but he did have to take time to go buy gumballs, go to the retail business, and fill the machine and go back to collect the profits. So that's not truly passive income.* You are kind of right—it's not totally passive income. However, the principle is correct. Whether Lucas got out of bed each day or not, his gumball machine was working for him.

Intellectual property is another form of passive income.

Musicians, actors, writers, and artists can all create passive income. They create from their heads a book, a song, a poem, a movie, a TV show, a picture, a photograph, a drawing, or a graphic of some kind. They create it once. However, one creation can be sold multiple times over, and over, and over again. For example, it could be in the form of a book, a t-shirt, whenever the song is played on the radio, or a rerun of a television show.

In the case of this book, although hundreds of hours were spent in the idea stage, writing and multiple edit stages, interviewing and writing of the kids' perspectives, and getting the book to market, once the book was completed, each one of us will get a tiny bit of passive income because you bought this book.

Our YET students didn't really have an idea of what passive income was when we approached them to participate; however, you can bet they have a better understanding each time they get a payment from the sale of every book sold! For them, this is truly a good example of what we have taught them. In addition to the term passive income, we also use the term, "mailbox money," as once the effort was completed, the cheque comes in the mail, over and over again.

No matter where you invest your money for it to grow, you will always need to take some time and look after the money. This is true for investments you have at the bank, stocks or shares you might own, or even a business venture you own and do not have to spend time working in.

True passive income happens when you are not required to show up at a pre-determined time to get paid. It does not mean that you can be totally passive. All money and investments will take some time for you to monitor and take care of.

One purpose for the money in your Wealth Jar is having money available for you to use to create your own passive income when the right opportunity comes your way.

Chapter 39
Passive Income and the Rat Race

We learned about the concept of passive income from Robert and Kim Kiyosaki and their board game called *CashFlow*. The game was intended to mirror the life most people lead in the civilized world. We all have choices come our way once we are working and everything we do impacts both our finances and our future.

The goal of the game is to create more monthly passive income (defined as cash flow from interest plus dividends plus real estate plus businesses) than monthly expenses.

Each player begins the game by randomly selecting a career card and a colored token shaped like a well-dressed rat to use as their game piece. The players then fill out their financial scorecard with the details of the salary, expenses, and debt as listed on the career card they have selected.

The game begins in a circle in the middle of the board game. At each turn in the game, dice are shaken to determine the number of squares the player will move around the circle. The circle is intended to represent the rat race most of us experience. Each stop along the circle offers a different action, including paydays, opportunities to invest or spend money, add children to your game life, and potentially experience a job layoff or divorce.

As the player lands on each of the squares, the choices they make will reflect their financial score card, including cash on hand, an increase or decrease in debt, or the amount of passive income they are earning.

Once the player reaches the point in the game where their passive income exceeds their monthly expenses, they are officially out of the rat race circle, and they move on to the outer perimeter of the board game where amazing lifestyle choices and generous donations to charity can be made and big business opportunities are located.

In our personal experience, the *Cashflow* game is a great reflection of the world we live in. Once we had the choice to remain working at our jobs or leave them and move onto other ventures, we found that multiple opportunities seemed to come our way in investments, businesses, ways to continue to grow our money, and the amount of money we had available to donate to charities and other worthwhile causes.

The *Cashflow* board game is a great way to identify how you handle your money in the real world. It gives you a risk-free idea of what is possible once you start to pay attention to your money and helps you understand how a Money Monster can both be tamed and used to your advantage.

Our intention in sharing this game with you is to encourage you to seek out an opportunity to play the game and help you understand our next topic, Wealth Ratios.

Norma: PS – Kids over the age of ten love to play *Cashflow* with adults. My ten-year-old grandson whipped my husband's butt and still loves to tell the tale! There is also a younger version of the game called *Cashflow for Kids* marketed for kids ages five through twelve; however, I found that by the age of ten, my grandkids were ready to move on to the adult version.

Chapter 40
Wealth Ratios

A wealth ratio is also a term we learned from Robert and Kim Kiyosaki. When your wealth ratio is greater than one, it means you are officially and financially able to leave the rat race of everyday life—if you choose to do so.

If you were to write this concept as a simple math formula it would look like this:

Passive Income / Expenses = Wealth Ratio

A wealth ratio of one or higher is your goal in life. Just like in the Cashflow board game, in the real world, when your passive income is higher than all the expenses in your life, you can choose to go to work each day or you can sit on a beach and sip mojitos! In short, you essentially could retire if that's what you want to do.

The reason we have given away copies of the book *Rich Dad, Poor Dad* is the concepts Robert Kiyosaki teaches are so very simple to understand, anyone can choose to implement them in their life. If you have already read the book and either missed or forgot the formula, we suggest you re-read it. There's a reason we are telling you this.

When we were younger, we both dreamed about having a million dollars in the bank and thought we would be rich and never work again. We have since learned in real life that is simply not true. If you do nothing with that million dollars to help it grow, inflation will outpace the money in the bank, you will eventually spend it all, and it will be gone. Then it's back to working at a job again.

After reading and truly understanding the concept of passive income, we realized we didn't need a million dollars. We just needed a wealth ratio of one or higher.

We are very grateful to say we reached this point in life and it is a very nice way to live.

We want the same opportunity for other people, including you and your children.

There are two ways to raise your wealth ratio. One is to earn more passive income, and the other is to reduce your expenses. It really is that simple!

In Chapter 32, we asked you to create a Spending Summary. One of its purposes was to help you identify areas in your life where you were spending your money and where you could potentially reduce your expenses. If you've completed this exercise, you will have already figured out there are only so many things you can do to reduce your day-to-day living costs.

For kids it's a different story. Kids don't start out in life with expenses. If you teach them about passive income at an early stage in life, they can begin to make smarter choices. When they see something, they want or will create an ongoing expense (like a cell phone bill), they can also choose to find or create a source of income to pay for that expense.

Can Passive Income Pay for a Ferrari?

One of the most interesting experiences and learning opportunities my husband Jeff and I had the chance to experience was attending a business conference in Arizona where Robert Kiyosaki lives and was one of the main speakers.

We were anticipating his arrival and several of us were watching for him to arrive. Would he arrive by limousine? Would he drive himself? What kind of car would he drive? A group of us were discussing these questions and more.

Soon we spotted a bright yellow Ferrari as it turned off the freeway and onto the side road. Was that Robert's car?

We all stood in awe as the man himself smoothly pulled into the parking lot and manoeuvred into a parking space. "Great car," someone remarked. "Exactly what I was expecting," said another.

Me? I said nothing, I thought he would have driven something less flashy and less expensive. After all, he teaches buying expensive toys—he calls them doodads—are foolish. I was confused.

During the conference we were given the opportunity to ask questions and talk with Robert. I bravely asked Robert if he would classify his Ferrari as a doodad.

Robert has a reputation of being "gruff" at times and I braced myself for his response. After all, I was being quite forward by questioning his choice of vehicles.

Thankfully, Robert started to laugh and said that was a great question. He then explained since he had earned enough cash from his businesses to buy the Ferrari, he was able to do so. I thought that would be the end of his explanation, but it was not.

Robert went on to explain he had learned to have his money work for him and he could also enjoy the benefits of managing his money. A Ferrari at the time was worth approximately

$250,000. He had the option to pay cash for the car—however, it was a doodad, not an asset, and would have been a bad decision.

Instead, he used $250,000 to invest in leveraged real estate, an apartment complex. The tenants in his buildings paid rent and after servicing the debt and paying all expenses on the real estate, he had enough money each month to make payments on the Ferrari.

By the time the Ferrari was paid for, it might be worth less money than he paid for it, but the apartment complex would be worth substantially more.

In the meantime, he had the fun and freedom of owning and driving a Ferrari. In addition, his car payments were a legitimate business expense, therefore reducing the taxes in his business and the payments were being made by the positive cash flow from his real estate. The moral of the story: You can have your Ferrari and
your apartment building too—if you chose to learn how

to manage your money and create passive income!

Having money in a Wealth Jar is the beginning of creating passive income opportunities.

We believe the Wealth Jar to be the most important jar in the Mmm system. It can provide funds for starting a small business if your kids are interested in becoming entrepreneurs, or it can be used as investment money to provide for their future wants and needs.

In a way, their wanted or needed item could become almost free to them in a sense. They don't have to get a job or go to work to get what they want—they may simply choose to put their Wealth Jar money to work instead.

Once kids understand passive income and how they can create it, they can strive to grow their Wealth Jars with the intention of using that money to create enough passive income to cover all their expenses for the rest of their lives.

Technically speaking, they may never have to work at a traditional job if they don't want to.

Learning to become a Money Master is smart. They can have a choice about how to live their lives. Not such a bad skill or mindset to learn, is it?

Imagine you could have worked by choice and not necessity. Think of all the time you could spend doing whatever it is that makes you happy. You could have spent more time learning—simply for the love of learning. You might have spent time caring for a loved one or building schools or homes for the underprivileged. True wealth is really all about having the choice regarding how to spend your time.

Can you imagine what a great gift this is to give the young people in your life? It's almost too good to be conceivable and yet it's true. It is possible. The good news is you know it's still achievable for you, too.

As adults with a high load of bad debt and a Money Monster at the door, it might be hard to believe you can shift your life to live this way. However, it is entirely possible. We know, because we've been in your shoes and we've made that shift.

It all starts with thinking differently, being open to learning and applying what we have shared and surrounding yourself with the right people. This brings us to our next chapter, Influence from Others.

Chapter 41
Influence from Others

We have learned our lives are directly impacted both emotionally and financially by the five people we spend the most time with. This is what we call your, "Circle of Six": you and the five friends you hang out with.

If you want to know where you are likely to end up financially, write down the names of those five people (outside your immediate family), what their primary source of income is (employee, self-employed, business owner, or investor), and your best guess as to what their annual income is. Divide that number by five, and we are betting you are in that same income bracket. That is the level of income where you will likely remain. It is also likely you will stay in the same source of income as those five.

Although a well-written and thought-provoking book can be the beginning of mentorship for you and help you to raise your level of income (providing you are willing to act on what you learn), the people in your life will have a greater impact on your success than you could imagine.

The people you spend the most time with are also mentors, by design or by default; they influence you in many ways. It doesn't mean they are great or not great people; it simply means you are most often influenced by the people you spend time with.

You can still spend time enjoying your friends' company. However, we want you to consider expanding the circle of people you hang out with.

Start looking for like-minded people who are also working toward the goal of getting "out of the rat race"—people who are positive in their thoughts and actions and who have the same values as you do.

Find people who know, understand, and practice this concept, and spend as much time with them as you can. We guarantee you will find yourself being pulled toward a better life, both financially and energetically.

Chapter 42
Finding a Personal Mentor

Most people who are successful in life usually like to help others find success, as well. Do not be intimated by people you think are richer or more successful than you. They all wake up in the morning and put their pants on one leg at a time, the same way as the rest of the world.

In our experience they are simply human beings with the same wants, needs, fears, and challenges as everyone else. They are approachable.

The one difference we have learned is most successful people intuitively know people; they can usually sense if others are looking to take advantage of them, or if people are genuine and kind in their hearts.

We can offer you this tip: Whenever you meet someone new that you find interesting, don't be intimidated by them. Ask them what makes them happy, or what project they are working on right now that makes them smile. People love to talk about themselves and about positive things. If you would like to get to know them better, ask if you can buy them a coffee or lunch sometime. Then follow-up in a timely way when they accept your offer.

If you approach them with the intent to get to know them better and not to simply suck their time or knowledge away, they will sense that and be more open to allowing you into their life. Be genuine and offer to help them when possible—simply for the opportunity to watch and learn more about who they are and what they do.

Don't forget—if you invited them for coffee or lunch, make sure you pay the check. Action and integrity are always rewarded. Make sure you thank them for their time and consider sending a follow-up thank-you card—in the mail (not email). You'll stand out above the crowd!

Chapter 43
It's Time to Teach Your Kids

We know we have given you a lot to think about. Based on our own experience, we know its not easy to look back at past decisions (especially the ones that didn't work out), adjust to a new action plan, and move forward toward a new way of thinking. However, we can tell you it feels fantastic once the decision is made and the steps required are put into motion.

We know you don't want your kids to struggle in life. This means it's now your turn to truly mentor and create a new reality for your children.

You've helped your kids to learn to walk and talk, brush their teeth every day and say please and thank you. You can also teach them permanent money management skills and have them love every minute of it.

We have simplified this entire book into the following steps to get you started.

1. Make a commitment you are going to become their money mentor.
2. Make the decision you are going to place money in their hands on a regular basis using either the "Allowance for Chores" or "Allowance for Money Management" method.
3. Decide how much money you will be able to consistently pay out on a go-forward basis at each Allowance Hour.
4. Gather enough jars for each person in your family, as well as some decorating items—colored markers, paints, felt cut-outs, pens, stickers, glue, paper, etc.
5. Call a family meeting and talk about what this book has meant to you and how you want all of you to have a better and easier financial life.
6. Review Chapter 9, "A Kid's Perspective on Money," and have a conversation with your

kids. Where do they think money comes from?

7. Review Chapter 10, "Where Does Money Come From?" Talk with your kids about those categories and let them know that you will be soon giving them money for a different purpose. Your purpose is to teach them to become Money Masters!

8. Talk to them about the Allowance Hour and how that is when they will receive their money; however, the money comes with rules and responsibility.

9. Choose the date and time for your Allowance Hour and go over the rules. We suggest you have a written sheet for all of you to sign once the rules are read and understood. You can then post that sheet in a place everyone can easily access. In many households, the fridge is a favorite location. Promise to make Allowance Hour fun!

10. Have a brief discussion on Chapter 11, "Managing Systems," and talk about how Mmm is the system they will be learning to

become Money Masters. The use of the jars is a part of that system.

11. Discuss how additional money (gift money and extra earned money) will be managed in the Mmm Jar System.
12. Explain to them you will be working alongside them to better your own money mastery skills and while you may not have all the answers to their questions about money, moving forward you will learn together as a family.
13. Briefly describe the categories in the Mmm System (Chapters 16–22) and explain they will each decorate and own a set of jars to use for dividing their money into the different categories.
14. Decide where the sets of jars will be kept and ensure that everyone understands they are not permitted to move money from jar to jar. Once it is placed in a category, it stays in that category.
15. Have fun decorating the jars and make sure to label them with the correct percentages

for each category, along with each child's name on each jar.

16. Reconfirm the next Allowance Hour time and place. Make sure you do this at the end of every Allowance Hour!

You can choose to have your first Allowance Hour right after the decorating of the jars, or within the next few days. Remember once you commit to a time and place, it is a COMMITMENT for the entire family. If someone cannot be present (other than because of illness), they are not paid their allowance.

As their Money Mentor, you need to be available, cash-in-hand and prepared with a topic for discussion for each meeting. You may wish to review Chapter 23 to prepare for the first few Allowance Hour meetings.

Additional resources are available on our website, and you may wish to join our Facebook Page for new ideas and to connect with like-minded people. Facebook is an easy to way to start increasing your own Circle of Six.

You can do this!

Chapter 44

The Mmm System and the YET Program —Kids' Perspectives

As you may very well have figured out by now, we are very proud of the YET program as well as the Money Master Management (Mmm) system and the difference it has already made in the kids we have worked with.

As we stated earlier, the first graduating students were invited to help write this book to assist them with the beginning stages of creating intellectual property that will translate to the beginnings of their own passive income.

The kids were a lot of fun to work with, both during the program and during the creation of this book. They had some of their own thoughts they wanted to share.

As we were writing and editing the book there did not seem to be a natural place to include their comments and thoughts, so we've decided to place them here and we encourage you to read through them.

Kai, Age Thirteen:

"When I first heard about the YET program, I was very confused. I didn't know what an entrepreneur was. As Lance explained the program a bit more and told us about the things we would learn, I began to understand.

In the first three weeks, I felt it was a bit boring and confusing, but my mom told me I had to go, and so I did. I also practised what I was learning, and then it began to be a lot of fun. I looked forward to going every week.

I liked learning new things, and now I think of business ideas all the time. I can think of new things to make and try, and I know I can do whatever I want if I just make the effort.

I use the Master Money System at home, and I really like it. I manage and look after my money, I know my limits on where I can spend and what I need to save, and it's easy to follow.

I think people should do the program—it's fun, it's easy, and you get to make your own money with a business. It also taught me to think outside the box. I know I liked building stuff, but it gave me the confidence to try things that were different. Now I explore a lot of ideas.

My latest business, the Fidgie Spinners, is starting out pretty well. I sold fifteen or so of them at the Women's Expo for $20 each, and the cost of goods to make them is around $5. I'm also looking at possibly selling them online or reselling another product line that is similar.

I like being able to manage my money. It's fun, not that hard, and allows me to do different things like put money away for expenses in my business and still have money for other stuff. I like that it keeps my money all organized; it's easy to find, and I know what to do with it. It gives me control and helps me with my math skills.

What I don't really like is that I have limits on money I can spend in any one area, so it sometimes takes a bit longer to get what I want. I'm OK with that; it is just sometimes a little frustrating.

I don't know what the future will bring, but I know that before the YET Program, it could have been a big struggle. Now that I've graduated, I can now see my future is going to be GREAT!"

Taya, Age Eleven:

"I was in the car driving with my mom when she told me about the YET program. I'm not a huge fan of math and was not all that excited at first. However, Mom kept explaining that it was about business and not just about math, so I become much more interested.

I found the program pretty fun right from the beginning, and I liked going every week. It was something I looked forward to. I had a lot of fun learning, and now that I am finished, I think *it was one of the best decisions I made in my whole life.*

I think the program is a really good idea because not that many teachers talk about business or teach about money. I like those topics.

I've continued to use the Jar System at home, and I love it. I have almost enough saved up to buy my own laptop. It's great, and the best part is that I don't spend all my money right away like I used to. There is no temptation to spend it all like before I learned how to manage my money. Back then I would also spend it almost as fast as I got it. Now I plan on how I want to spend money on the things I want, but I still have money to play with, too. It's pretty easy; I like it.

I definitely think kids should take the program. It's a good learning experience, and it's a really fun thing to do. I think I have a better understanding and use of my money compared to most of my friends. I sometimes have to ask my parents for money, but not often. I have my own money to spend, and it makes me feel good not to have to ask my parents for money.

I don't know what my future is going to bring, but a lot of people think I'm going to go places because I'm not afraid to talk to anyone anymore. I used to be kind of shy. I know I want to start my own business of some kind, and I might become a marine biologist, too. I have the confidence to do both if I want."

Shaqala, Age Fifteen:

"When I first heard about the YET Program, I thought it was a cool idea. I was interested in making my own business, so I wanted to try it out. It was quite fun, and I normally don't like doing things that I'm not that familiar with. Now that I'm finished, I would encourage people to check it out, it was a great experience for me, and I use the skills I learned every day.

I'm very happy I took the program. Lance taught me a lot of things I would never have learned in school. It helped me to look at money and business in a different, better way. It taught me to save money for stuff that I actually need and not just want.

In the past, I would spend all my money on candy and clothes, and my bank would always be empty. Now I have lots more money, and when I go shopping, I make decisions on do I need this or do I want this. Sometimes I buy stuff because I want it, but I think about it more. Most of my friends just spend without thinking and then complain they are broke.

The best part is that I don't need to ask my parents for money anymore. Recently, my mom and I went shopping at Winners and I picked out some rugs for my room. My mom thought she would have to pay for them, but I decided I wanted to. Mom was surprised, but I felt proud that I could pay for my own things.

I'm not sure what the future will bring. My photography business is starting to take off pretty good; I was asked to do a wedding shoot this summer, which is a job worth between $500 to $700—not bad for a kid!

Right now, I'm saving up for a car for when I turn sixteen. I'd like to buy an electric car, like a Volt. They cost a lot, but I've already saved up around $3,000 or so.

I have big dreams. Someday I would like to live in California and be a photographer; I would live in a penthouse and own a Lamborghini. I don't know if that is going to happen or not, but I do know that I am now very self-confident. Before YET I didn't like talking to people, especially large groups of people. I can speak confidently now in front of anyone, so anything is possible—even my big dream ☺.*"*

Kamryn, Age Ten:

"When I first heard about the YET program, I was very excited, but also very nervous. I would be the youngest kid there; I was only eight-years-old. I was worried that I would be a bit slow compared to the other kids. After a couple of weeks, I really looked forward to each new

lesson. I was doing really well in the program, and I felt good about myself.

I think everyone should do the program. It's a good learning experience to help people become more successful than trying to do that on their own. I feel like I got an opportunity in life that most kids don't, and I'm really happy I did the work. I've been using the Mmm system for almost two years now, and I know that I will keep doing that, even as an adult. I won't get caught up in debt because I can manage my money, and I know I can still have money to spend on myself when I want.

The hardest part is when you get like $100 and you can't go spend it all at the mall because you must manage it into the jars, but I know my friends don't have a system, and they blow their money all the time. I use the jars, and I feel good about it. Sometimes I need to ask my parents for money, but I usually have my own money with me. They always make me pay them back—and I'm OK with that.

I have learned that you should try and hang out with people who are doing better than you and are smarter than you, and not to let other people pull you down. I heard a story about how if you put a bunch of lobsters in a pot, they can't get out—because they keep pulling each other down. I want to tell people: Don't be lobsters! Be with other people who will lift you up, and then you can help other people get lifted, too.

When I grow up I want to help people or animals. I think I'll be a very successful person, and I will likely have money work for me."

From Lance and Norma:

The words above are directly from the kids and we are so very proud of each one of them. If you would like to connect with the kids and have your thoughts heard, visit us on our Facebook page and post your comments there. The kids will be watching! Our Facebook page is Money Monster or Money Master?

Chapter 45

Final Thoughts

Our Goal is to Make a Difference

Money is always going to be a part of our lives. We have learned it is so much better to have power over our money than to allow money to have power over us.

Teaching our kids to handle money responsibly while they are young sets them up for success in life. If you are reading this book, it is because you care.

Take pride and joy in knowing they—and you—will be better off in the future, because you can learn and teach them a way to be successful with money, so they will never need to tame a Money Monster of their own. With your help and guidance, neither money nor credit need to be a source of problems in their lives.

We both want to help make people's lives better and happier. We've seen life doesn't have to be as hard as what we've been taught or think it is. A few basic principles around money management can change a person's life forever.

Our goal is to make a difference and we know that you, our readers, are the stepping-stones to changing the world as we have known it. Thank you. You are appreciated and in our daily thoughts of gratitude.

Parting Thoughts from Norma

Two of my core values are communication and empowerment. When I first met Lance, we immediately connected energetically, and a wonderful friendship began to grow. As Lance started to dream about creating the YET program for kids, my heart swelled with excitement.

His initial goal was to make a difference locally in his own community. I saw a bigger picture and knew with the right team, vision, and hard work, his program could impact the world.

Writing and sharing this book and promoting the YET program fulfills my core values. The more we communicate on these topics, the more people can be empowered to make a difference in the world around them.

The days are long past that anyone can rely on governments and traditional school systems to fully educate our children. It is entrepreneurial thinking that creates jobs and it is good money management habits that will create financial freedom for both entrepreneurs and employees. We need to help more people see and understand those options and know they are completely within their power to be, do, or have anything their heart desires.

Every generation wants a better world for their children than the generation before them. I have learned this is true in every country and culture I have had the opportunity to visit. Ultimately, I believe teaching and sharing is like throwing a stone into the water—it has a ripple effect. It is my hope that as this book is shared, each person we reach will begin to have a healthier, happier, and more fulfilled life of choice, not chance.

My final words are of gratitude. I am grateful to my entire family. This includes the family members I am close with and the family members with whom I choose to no longer have contact with. I have had both many heart-filled moments and times of heartache from each and every one of them. It is with genuine gratitude I thank them from the bottom of my heart, for they have helped me grow into the woman I am today.

I am grateful for my friends—simply for being my best cheerleaders and allowing such an expanded Circle of Six to impact my life.

I am forever grateful for the opportunity to work with our team and especially for Lance, who holds a special place in my heart. Each one of you has made a positive difference in my life.

And finally, I am grateful for my husband Jeff, who has always been kind, loving, and supportive in every aspect of my life. I love him more today than yesterday and never as much as I know I will love him tomorrow.

Parting Thoughts from Lance

As my fifteen-year-old son stood on stage as the opening speaker in Las Vegas in front of 650 CEOs from around the world, I was so very proud. I knew no matter what he chose to do in life, he would be OK. He was a young man filled with compassion, charisma, and confidence, yet he was humble enough to be grateful for the opportunity to be there. I knew I had taught him the basics in life he would need to be successful. I had done my job as a parent.

After his presentation, many of the CEOs approached me to ask me how I raised Lucas to be so well-spoken and confident and I thought to myself, *It was my job—isn't that what parents are supposed to do?* As parents, these very successful and influential people wanted the same skills and confidence for their own children, but they told me they didn't know what or how to teach their own kids.

I was taught if enough people ask the same question or have a similar problem, there is both an opportunity and an obligation to find a solution. As more and more people started to ask me about Lucas, it finally sunk in. I could help parents by sharing what I had done with my own children.

As the idea of the Young Entrepreneur Training (YET) program developed in my mind, I began to get excited at the thought that perhaps I could reach a couple hundred families and their kids, and I could make a difference in my own community. I shared my enthusiasm and goal with friends and family. It was Norma who said to me, "Lance, I know you said a couple hundred kids, but I think you're missing a number of zeros on the end of that." She helped me to realize my program and goal to help kids didn't need to be limited to those close to me—and together we could help kids all around the world.

We strategized on how to start reaching and teaching the basics of what parents need to do for their children, how best to inspire them to believe in themselves and develop money, business, social, and life skills in a fun and easy way, so each child could fully reach their own individual potential.

She helped me see this book could become the starting point for many families and how the YET program would be a continuation for those that see themselves as wanting more in life than just getting a job and being at the mercy of employers and government programs.

Jobs and businesses may come and go. Life circumstances will change over time. However, when kids have been empowered with knowledge and real-life skills, they can face both opportunity and adversity with an advantage many people will never have. The skills and confidence the kids acquire through this book and YET program is permanent and can never be taken away from them. Kids are our future and I'm excited to know we can and will positively impact the world to be a better and kinder place.

I've been asked, "When will you know if the YET program is a success?" The truth is, I really don't know how to answer that question and I likely won't know anytime soon. I can share with you when I saw my first group of YET grads stand on stage in front of people and confidently speak about their businesses and themselves, my heart swelled, and my eyes teared up. Those kids could barely stop smiling; they simply beamed with confidence and pride in themselves.

Self-esteem can be seen when you build it in a child. I've done it. I've seen it. I felt successful in each of those moments. I want other parents to feel that same success and knowing that will happen is a part of my success, but that itself can never be measured.

At some point in my life, all I truly want is for someone to approach me and say, "Mr. Dinahan, I was fortunate in my life someone cared enough about me to teach me what you have shared. I see others struggle, but I do not simply because of what I have learned through you. I just wanted to say thank you—because of you, I can now help others in a way I never dreamed."

Dreaming is important. My dream is to help more kids than I can ever imagine or possibly count in my lifetime. Another big dream is to someday be on *The Ellen DeGeneres Show*. Not for my own fame, but because I know she can help me reach more kids. I believe she has the same heart as I do—we both love to make people laugh and we both love kids. I want to thank her in person, for what she does for others.

You may only be one person and so am I, but collectively if we each do our best to share what we know, we can change the world. I want you to share what you learn in this book to help kids. Don't just read the book and put it on a shelf. I want you to engage with the kids in your life and help them become the best human beings they can be.

Can you imagine a world where generations of kids can go through life, "Striving to Make a Difference Rather Than Striving to Make a Dollar"? I can, and I hope I have inspired you to make that dream happen.

Thank you from me personally for being willing to pick up and read this book, for considering my YET program, and for wanting to make a difference in someone's life.

I wish you prosperity and happiness in all that you do.

All the best,

Lance Dinahan

Dedication

I dedicate this book to my three children, Tiana, Lucas, and Aisha. Since the day they were born, they have been my inspiration to always be a better me. The first time I laid my eyes on them, I knew my life was no longer for me but was now for them.

To my extended and blended family, including Kai, Taya, Jordyn, Kamryn, Nik and all the other kids who have taken the YET program, I consider you, "my kids," as well. I know you will use the skills and knowledge you have learned to make your life and the lives of those around you much better.

To Norma, for making me realize my dream was a little too small and together we could be the ones to make the bigger difference in the world.

Lastly, to my family and friends (too many to list) for always being there and putting up with me. To each of you who believed in me, encourage me and even lifted me back up again when I've fallen, you have been truly a blessing in my life. While I always do my best to make you laugh and smile with me, you may think I've made your lives better, but the truth is, it has been ALL of you who have made my life better.

    Love to all of you,

    Lance

Acknowledgments

One of my core values is communication, the other is empowerment. I felt passionate about making this book the best that it could be. Little did I know how much time and hard work it would take to put words to paper and get to the publishing stage.

Lance and I both believe in mentors and coaches and creating a "Circle of Six". People in which we can learn and grow with, laugh and share moments of despair, but most of all, simply keep things moving. This book would not have happened without our "Circle of Six" of support.

I would like to acknowledge Alex Carroll who insisted I listen to a Webinar with David Chilton. Alex told me it would help me write a Best Seller book, and I believed him.

I would also like to thank David Chilton, who accepted an email I sent to him in gratitude and called me back that very same day. It was through David's online program about writing and marketing, combined with his personal encouragement by phone and emails that kept me going during some of the toughest times of writing, testing, re-testing and re-writing.

Although I had hired and paid a professional editor, it was Dr. Vicki Panaccione who voluntarily stepped up and edited, the editor's version. This book would not be the same without her help. I feel blessed to have had her dedication to perfection.

Finally, to my friend Kelly Woodhouse Falardeau, who patiently helped me with the technical challenges of getting the book onto Amazon and Kindle. Without Kelly – this book would have taken another 3 months of stress and tears.

There were so many people who encouraged us along the way. To each of you, a BIG HUG, and a HEARTY THANK YOU!

Norma

Part 7

Additional Resources and Information

In the ever-changing world of technology, resources, information, and support, opportunities are ever-changing. Our goal with making this book available was to help make a better future for both kids and adults. We hope you will take advantage of the resources we currently have, listed below, and future resources as they become available.

- FREE Bi-Monthly Newsletter
- FREE Downloadable Spending Sheet Summary
- FREE Allowance Hour Rules Agreement and Guide
- FREE Template to Make "Debit and Credit Cards"

Additionally, we will continue to recommend other relevant books, games and websites of which will be made available through links on our website.
Please visit us at

www.MoneyMonsterorMoneyMaster.com

Social Media:

Facebook Page: Money Master or Money Monster

Facebook Page: YET – Young Entrepreneurs Training

FREE Money Master Newsletter

Join us at www.MoneyMonsterOrMoneyMaster.com to sign up for our FREE bi-monthly newsletter, where we will provide additional ideas, tips and tricks to working with your kids to help them (and you) become financially free.

OUR PROMISE:

We WILL make it a maximum of one page in length and super easy and fun to read.
We will NOT sell, give away, or otherwise distribute your email address to anyone else.
And finally, ...

We WILL make it easy to unsubscribe, should you wish to do so at any time, although why you would want to unsubscribe to such a cool newsletter would be hard for us to understand!

                Signed: Lance Dinahan

                         Norma LaFonte

Money Master Book— BONUS

As our Thank You for purchasing and reading our book, we would like to gift you with a BONUS of six (6) months of access to our private Money Master Community Facebook Group for absolutely FREE, when you sign up for a one-year membership to our group!

Our private Money Master Facebook Group is a community of like-minded people who share not only their successes, but also their tips, tricks, trials and tribulations in helping their children find success. We feature stories and articles which will inspire both you and your children to continue using the Money Master Management (Mmm) System and support your role as their Mentor.

Simply send an email to: Bonus@MoneyMonsterorMoneyMaster.com

In the SUBJECT line state: Money Master Book BONUS

ATTACH: a picture of your book receipt (presuming you purchased this copy)—or you can provide your signature on the dotted line below, and then attach a scan or photo of this page to the email.

We will then return your email with a PERSONALIZED BONUS CODE for use when you subscribe, which will provide you with an additional FREE six-month subscription. This BONUS CODE may be used yourself or given to a friend or family member.

_____

Your Signature Please

This offer is open to all purchasers of *Money Monster or Money Master?* by Lance Dinahan and Norma LaFonte. Limit of one Personalized Bonus Code per copy of *Money Monster or Money Master?* by Lance Dinahan and Norma LaFonte, and subject to the online availability of the Private Money Master Community Facebook Group. Additional taxes or fees may apply at the time of registration, subject to the laws of where you reside.

Young Entrepreneur Training (YET)

Our Vision:

To Inspire People to Believe in Themselves

Our Mission:

To make a difference in the world by empowering people with business, social, and life skills. Young Entrepreneur Training (YET) will develop confidence that leads to success and prosperity.

Our Values:

Service
Honor
Respect
Responsibility
Accountability

www.YetTraining.com

Young Entrepreneur Training (YET)

Young Entrepreneurs Training (YET) is currently an international online training program created for people ages eight and up. The program assists kids, parents, and other adults who either want a simple way to understand how to start their own business and/or help the young people in their lives to be able to do so.

Lots of well known entrepreneurs reached their success by trial and error. It's not an easy path and not always a straight line to success. It takes hard work. But what if there were steps that could be taken that would make the journey quicker or easier? Would that be worth considering?

The problem most new entrepreneurs have is they don't boil their success down to basics. The YET program teaches the basics of success in such a way as to ensure they become lifelong skills and habits.

The online program contains over twenty professional training videos to help both the adult and the young person learn. Half of the videos are intended for the adult to view first and guide them to what the lesson is about and how to best support their young person in the topic being covered.

The other half of the videos are designed to watch together and can be viewed repeatedly until the concepts are clearly understood and implanted for permanent future success.

Some of the topics covered in the modules are: money and business basics, how to dress for success, and how to properly introduce themselves, the basics of selling, marketing, advertising, relationships, networking, and starting a business are also included. The program is supplemented with a workbook and a flash card game (which will be sent directly to your mailing address postage paid by us) to make the learning fun and really reinforce these life lessons.

Students also learn how to overcome one of the greatest fears in life: they will learn to feel confident and comfortable with public speaking. This is a skill that will serve them no matter which path in life they choose to take.

Students of the YET program work at their own pace and when the program is completed, they will have their very own business with sales, profits, and money in hand. The skills learned are not specific to any business model and may be adapted to any type of business the student may have an interest in. There are no limits as to what they may choose to do.

We're sure you have heard the expression, "Give a person a fish and they eat for a day; teach them to fish and they will eat for a lifetime." This program is not about giving a one-time experience. It is intended to ensure a lifetime of good habits and skills.

Have You Considered Your Children's Future YET?

www.YetTraining.com